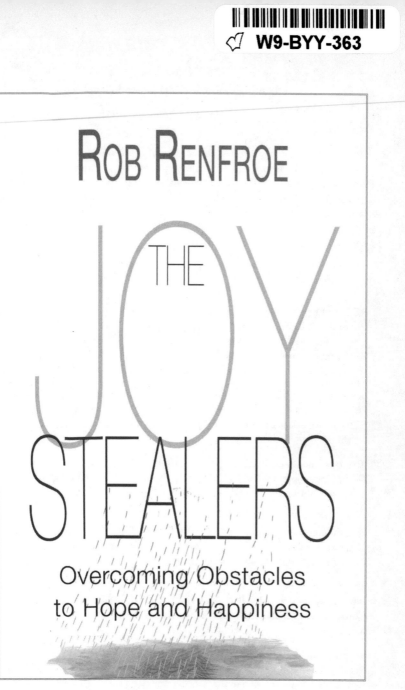

ROB RENFROE

THE JOY STEALERS

Overcoming Obstacles to Hope and Happiness

Abingdon Press / Nashville

There's within my heart
a melody

The Joy Stealers
Overcoming Obstacles to Hope and Happiness

ISBN 9781501857997

CONTENTS

INTRODUCTION

God's will for you is joy. By *joy* I mean a sense of well-being that is not dependent on good fortune, positive circumstances, or the blessing of an optimistic disposition. It's something much deeper and more enduring than the fleeting feelings of happiness we experience when "all's right with the world." God's desire for you is a sense of confidence and encouragement that transcends your situation because it is founded on your relationship with him.

Jesus taught this truth when he said he had revealed the Father's will for our lives "so that my joy may be in you and that your joy may be complete" (John 15:11).

The good news that Christians proclaim is that God loves us so much that he sent his Son into the world so we might have eternal life in the future AND so we could have abundant life in the here and now (John 10:10 NRSV). And part of that abundance is experiencing the same joy that Jesus knew.

Years ago I heard a comedian say, "Some people see the glass half full. Others see it half empty. Me? I keep wondering who's been drinking out of my glass."

When it comes to the joy you were meant to experience, does it ever feel like someone or something has been drinking out of your glass? Are there past hurts you can't shake? Does guilt drain your joy? Are there problematic relationships that won't change, or financial worries that hover over your future like ominous storm clouds? Is it the negative way you learned to look at life from your family of origin? Or maybe a "measure-up mentality" that tells you that you don't deserve to enjoy life until you've done one more thing?

Worry, bitterness, negativity, busyness and guilt—they will all steal our joy—but only if we let them.

I was taught what I believe to be the most important lesson about living with joy from a remarkable man thirty years ago. Danny was the most energetic, "in-love-with-life" person I have ever known. Seventy years old when I, as a young man, was his pastor in a small east Texas town, he never slowed down. He was always going somewhere, helping someone, taking on some new project to serve the God he loved.

I once mentioned Danny to a church member, who had known him for years. "I wouldn't mind doing the way Danny does when I'm seventy," I said. Matter-of-factly he replied, "Rob, you don't do as much as he does now. How are you going to get better over the next forty years?"

Danny was a sought-after Bible teacher who spoke all over the state. He took care of several homebound senior citizens, making certain they were eating properly, getting to their doctor's appointments, and paying their bills. He served on several church committees and oversaw the personal finances of one of the wealthiest men in Texas. Somehow, he also found time to build our sons a playhouse in the backyard that they enjoyed for years. And he did it all with boundless energy, an infectious spirit, and a huge smile that never quit.

On a church trip, I sat next to him, knowing I would have two hours to talk with him. I thought, "This is my chance. Maybe I can learn something from him about living the way he does." So, I asked Danny to tell me the story of his life.

What I learned that day I have never forgotten. It just wasn't what I expected.

Danny's father had been killed in a car accident when Danny was young. His sister had disappeared when she was in her early twenties. No one had ever heard from her again. His mother died in a little East Texas hospital because of a botched operation. His granddaughter had died of a rare disease when she was only two. And his wife, the love of his life for the past fifty years, was suffering with the cancer that would later take her life.

When he finished speaking, it took me a few moments to process all he had said. Finally, I asked, "Danny, having been through so much, how can you live the way you do?" His answer was as profound as it was simple. "Rob, I decided a long time ago that I wasn't going to let anything take away the joy that is mine in Jesus Christ."

The first three words of his answer have always stayed with me. "Rob, I decided."

That day I learned from Danny that joy is a decision. In Christ, we have everything we need for joy—the forgiveness of our sins, the indwelling of the Holy Spirit, a purpose worth living for, and the assurance of eternity with God. But whether we live with joy or let something take it from us, that's a choice each of us makes. Often, choosing joy is not easy. What makes it even more difficult is that it's a decision we must make over and over. If it were as simple as flipping a switch, we'd all be happy all the time.

But living with joy is a decision we must make and remake when our circumstances and our relationships and our brokenness threaten to take away the joy that is ours in Jesus Christ.

When we are worried and anxious, we can choose to cast our cares upon him (1 Peter 5:7). And we can live with joy.

When we have been wounded and hurt by the actions of others to the point that bitterness begins to poison our souls, we can choose to forgive and as a result be healed and set free.

When we have been disappointed by life or let down by others and we find ourselves becoming negative and cynical, we can decide that the state of our souls will be determined not by what happens to us but by what happens in us.

When we discover ourselves to believe that our worth is found in doing enough for others that they love us and praise us, we can determine that our sense of self will be found in who God says we are, not what others think about us.

When we struggle to measure up to some ideal we have in our heads or with who others told us we should be when we were growing up, we can choose to open our lives to the incredible grace of God that frees us from a life of constantly striving to be something we're not.

We can make these decisions. None of them is easy. Most of them require self-understanding, a commitment to personal responsibility, and a process of emotional and spiritual growth. But to live with joy, these decisions must be made. The good news is that with God's help we can make them.

What follows are five chapters, each one describing a "joy stealer" and its effect on our lives, as well as some practical, biblical advice on how to overcome each one. The final chapter looks at the life of Paul–a man who lived with remarkable joy in spite of incredible problems—and what we can learn from his example.

My prayer is that God will use this book to help you step into the abundant life that is ours in Jesus Christ.

1

WORRY

"*Therefore I tell you, do not worry about your life, what you will eat or drink; or about your body, what you will wear. Is not life more than food, and the body more than clothes? Look at the birds of the air; they do not sow or reap or store away in barns, and yet your heavenly Father feeds them. Are you not much more valuable than they? Can any one of you by worrying add a single hour to your life?*

"*And why do you worry about clothes? See how the flowers of the field grow. They do not labor or spin. Yet I tell you that not even Solomon in all his splendor was dressed like one of these. If that is how God clothes the grass of the field, which is here today and tomorrow is thrown into the fire, will he not much more clothe you— you of little faith? So do not worry, saying, 'What shall we eat?' or 'What shall we drink?' or 'What shall we wear?' For the pagans run after all these things, and your heavenly Father knows that you need them. But seek first his kingdom and his righteousness, and all these things will be given to you as well. Therefore do not worry about tomorrow, for tomorrow will worry about itself. Each day has enough trouble of its own."*

(Matthew 6:25-34)

A close friend had a son who was addicted to heroin. He loved his son more than he loved life, but the young man blamed his father, and to a lesser extent his mother, for his problems. And he shut them out of his life. For several months, they did not know where he was or even if he was alive. Every moment, my friend said, was filled with anxiety to the point that it was physically painful. Questions would race through his mind. How was his son? Was he safe? Did he have a place to stay? Was he hungry? Would they ever have a relationship again?

My friend told me that every time the phone rang, he would jump up, hoping it was his son. But as he raced to the phone, "the closer I got," he said, "there was the fear that it might not be my son but the sheriff asking me to identify a body. My heart would be gripped with fear and my hands would shake as I reached for the phone."

Then he said, "Rob, if I knew that he was going to be OK, I could bear this pain. If I was sure things were going to be all right, even if it took years, I could live with this. But I don't know how this will end. Sometimes I hurt so bad, I don't think I can take it another day."

Pressures at work, concerns about our family, health issues we or loved ones are facing, financial burdens, broken relationships—life places terrible burdens on us and makes no promises that the worst will not happen, that one day everything will turn out right. So we worry. We become anxious and stressed. And we wonder how we will ever experience a moment of peace, much less joy.

Some of us are anxious by nature. It's normal for us to worry. Maybe we learned it from a parent, or maybe that's just the way our internal chemistry works. Either way, we find that our minds seem to have a mind of their own. Even when we tell them not to, our minds begin to play out every situation that could happen, including everything that could possibly go wrong. We worry about what we did or said in the past. We worry about what's happening in the present. We worry about what might occur in the future. For some of us, worry is our "set point" and it's miserable.

I have known men and women who have been huge successes in their professional lives for years, including executives of large companies, yet who are wracked with the fear of being "found out." They think, one day they're going to figure out that I'm not as good as they think I am. They'll discover that I'm not all that smart or competent, that the only reason I succeed is because I work harder than others." This kind of fear strikes at our sense of self and produces incredible stress and anxiety.

Tom Hanks is one of our finest and most successful actors. He has received two Oscars for best actor in a leading role. His skills range from the comedic genius of Forrest Gump to the heroic everyman of Captain Miller in *Saving Private Ryan* to American attorney James Donovan in the espionage thriller *Bridge of Spies*. His annual earnings are reportedly around $26 million.[1] But even with that record of success, he stated in an NPR interview:

> No matter what we've done, there comes a point where you think, "How did I get here? When are they going to discover that I am, in fact, a fraud and take everything away from me?" . . . There are days when I know that 3 o'clock tomorrow afternoon I am going to have to deliver some degree of emotional goods, and if I can't do it, that means I'm going to have to fake it. . . . If

I fake it, that means they might catch me at faking it, and if they catch me at faking it, well, then it's just doomsday.[2]

Does Tom Hanks need to worry about not performing, not measuring up, or being exposed as "not having what it takes"? Of course not. But he does. Just like so many of us do. And that kind of stress is painful. It transforms the life God wants us to live—a joyful and challenging adventure—into a burden to bear.

I have discovered that people will do almost anything to get out of pain. When we are stressed and anxious, we often make big mistakes in how we try to find peace and joy. Some of us use alcohol to numb the pain. Or we become dependent on drugs, prescription or otherwise. Some turn to food or to pornography or to an affair to change how we feel. A typical pattern is to sit in front of the TV or the computer, shut down emotionally, and become unavailable to our friends, spouses, or children.

I don't know what God has in mind for you for the future. But I know he wants to use you for something important and good either in the lives of your loved ones or in the world in the name of Christ. But you will not be available to God if you handle your stress in ways that are destructive. And you will not know the joy that you were created to experience.

That's because when we try to solve a spiritual problem with a physical solution (and in just a moment we'll see that's what worry is), it never leads to happiness and wholeness. It only creates more dysfunction in our lives, more disconnectedness in our relationships, and more pain in our souls—in other words, more to worry about.

What is worry, and what does it do to us? The Latin word from which we derive the word *anxiety* means "to choke."[3] The Anglo-Saxon root for *worry* means "to strangle."[4] And that's what worry does. It chokes the life out of us. It strangles our ability to make good decisions. It cuts us off from others and spiritually makes us diseased. We know this intuitively. That's why we have expressions such as "he was worried sick" and "she was worrying herself to death."

What experience tells us, scientific research now confirms. Anxiety not only does nothing positive for us, but it's actually dangerous and destructive. Physically, anxiety can lead to hypertension, heart disease, and a compromised immune system. It can depress our appetite and disrupt our sleep. Emotionally, it can make us irritable and unstable, unable to see our problems with the perspective we need to make good, rational decisions. Relationally, worry can cause us to become impatient and strike out at others who have nothing to do with the problems we're facing. Spiritually, anxiety can cause us to lose sight of God and see nothing but problems.

Jesus spoke at length about worry in the Sermon on the Mount. He begins by saying, "Do not worry about your life" (Matthew 6:25), and he concludes his discourse with, "Do not worry about tomorrow, for tomorrow will worry about itself. Each day has enough trouble of its own" (Matthew 6:34).

It's easy to misunderstand this passage. Jesus is not saying that we don't need to plan ahead. Worrying about something and making plans for the future are two very different things. What he is saying is that worry will strangle our spirits and steal our joy. But more than that, Jesus is promising that there is a better way to go through life than being wracked with anxiety and fear.

How do we do that? In Matthew 6:25-34, Jesus tells us how. In this passage, Jesus gives us three descriptions of worry, and with each description, he gives us a prescription for overcoming anxiety and living with joy. Let's look at each one together.

Description #1: Worry Is a Faith Issue

Jesus says, "Look at the birds of the air; they do not sow or reap or store away in barns, and yet your heavenly Father feeds them. Are you not much more valuable than they?" (Matthew 6:26). In these two simple sentences, he clearly seems to be saying, "You do what the birds don't do. You sow, reap, and store your goods. If the Father provides for creatures who don't work and plan for the future, how much more certain you can be that God will take care of your needs." Of course, birds don't overspend or go into debt to buy stuff they don't need. But the point is that if God can meet the needs of the birds who have to go out and find food every day, then certainly he can provide for us who have the ability to work, save, and invest for the future.

Later in the passage Jesus tells us to consider the flowers in the field.

They don't labor or spin. But "if that is how God clothes the grass of the field, which is here today and tomorrow is thrown into the fire, will he not much more clothe you—you of little faith?" (Matthew 6:30). Did you catch that last phrase? "You of little faith." When do we worry? When our faith is small.

The church I serve has a heart for missions. A commitment to making the world better for people who are poor and who are without a saving knowledge of Jesus is at the core of who we are. One reason for that commitment is our missions pastor, Dr. John Hull. John and I are close friends, but on a mission trip we could hardly be more different.

I'm a worrier by nature. As a first-born perfectionist, I feel responsible for just about everything and possess a need to control what's happening—you know, for the good of others. We've taken as many as one hundred men at a time to some of the poorest and most dangerous cities in the world to construct churches, provide medical care, and build houses for families living in hovels made out of cardboard and scraps of wood.

Everything can be going well and yet there I am fretting and worrying about a dozen things that could go wrong. And when we have an actual problem—there aren't enough supplies to finish the project or we're shaken down at the border for a bribe and told we can't enter the country—I go running to John, saying, "This is terrible. What are we going to do? All these guys are depending on us." At that point John gets a big smile on his face and says, "Calm down. This is when God comes through and does his best stuff." How can John not become alarmed and anxious when things are going bad? To me, if you're not worried, it's because you don't care. To John, if you are worried, it's because you don't trust God. "You of little faith."

Before John started leading mission teams all over the world, he served seven years as a missionary in the Mexican desert. He lived alone in a trailer that wasn't weatherproofed and didn't have hot water. In those seven years, he established a medical clinic, built a hospital, and provided vacation Bible school for thousands of kids, never certain of where his funding would come from.

John has been in enough situations where he needed God to come through, trusted God to come through, and saw God come through that, when I'm anxious about all kinds of things, he's anxious for nothing—or pretty close to it.

The truth is you can put two people in identical circumstances, and one will worry and one will not. That's because worry is determined more by our internal condition than our external situation. We worry not when our problems are big but when our faith is small. If there is little faith within us, the smallest concerns will fill our hearts with great anxiety. But if we are full of faith, there will be little room for fear to take hold.

So, how do we keep from worrying? We can tell ourselves not to do something, but rarely is that enough. The best way to overcome a negative habit is to replace it with a healthy habit. And Jesus tells us how to do that in this same passage.

Prescription #1: Remind Yourself Who God Is

If worry is a faith issue, how do you increase your faith? You remember who God is. Jesus said, "Look at the birds of the air; they do not sow or reap or store away in barns, and yet your heavenly Father feeds them. Are you not much more valuable than they?" (Matthew 6:26). Jesus says that God is "your heavenly Father." You are valuable to him, he knows what you need, and he will provide for your needs.

God loves you. That is the truest truth about you—not what you have done, not the mistakes you've made, not what your past says about you, not the names that others have placed on you, and not the circumstances that surround you. And because God cares about you the way a truly loving father cares for his children, Jesus says that you can be sure he will provide for you.

Several years ago, I dropped by a member's home unannounced. He had been laid off when his company downsized, and I thought I would try to encourage him and his wife. They were surprised to see me but graciously invited me inside. Maybe I should have begun with, "So, Bill, I heard you lost your job," but I thought I'd let him bring it up.

"You guys were on my mind," I said. "How are y'all doing?"

"We're doing great," he responded.

Hmm, I tried again. "How are things?"

Same answer: "Everything's going good."

Finally, I got to it. "Bill, I heard you were laid off, and I came by because I care about y'all and wanted to make sure you're OK."

He chuckled. Honestly, he laughed. And with a big smile on his face he said, "Brother Rob, Judy and I are going to be fine. My job was my provision. But God is my Provider. My provision has changed, but my Provider has not."

Why was Bill at peace? Because he wasn't looking at his circumstances, his job, or his provision. His eyes were on his Provider, his God, his heavenly Father who loved him. His situation had changed, but his source of provision, peace, and joy had not. He believed that the unchanging God who had proven himself faithful in the past would prove himself faithful in the future.

Paul writes in 2 Corinthians, "It is by faith you stand firm" (1:24). That's why two people in identical circumstances can say two different things. One will say, "My situation is overwhelming," and the other will say, "My Savior is sovereign." One will think, "My circumstances say . . ." and the other will proclaim, "The word of God says . . ." One will live worried and afraid; the other will live in faith and joy. One will fall, and one will stand firm.

That's because, ultimately, worry is not determined by whether we have problems. It's determined by whether we have faith.

How do we get more faith? In the Book of Romans, Paul tells us the answer: "So faith comes from hearing, and hearing through the word of Christ" (Romans 10:17 ESV).

In times of crisis and anxiety, it's important that we get into the word and that we get the word into us, because God's word has the power to create within us faith and life and strength. If we want to stand firm and live with joy, we need to hear the word, read the word, and fill our minds with the word.

If you focus on your problems, become obsessed with the bad news that surrounds you, and lift your eyes no higher than your circumstances, you will walk through life defeated and despairing. But if you focus on God and his promises, you will walk with confidence and peace and be able to overcome anxiety.

Who is God? He is your loving Father who has promised to be your provider. He knows what you need materially. He is aware of your need for friendship and relationships that provide comfort and strength. He, even more than you, knows how desperately you need his presence in your life. He knows and cares about the places in your life that require healing and restoration.

You are valuable to God. You are dear to his heart. He sent Jesus into the world to die on the cross because even though he had everything that existed, he did not have you. Now that God has made you his own, you can be sure that he will provide for you.

Read God's word. Claim his promises. Trust his provision. Whatever the problem you're facing may be, he knows and cares. And he will provide what you need.

Description #2: Worry Is Foolishness

After talking about trusting God to provide for our needs, Jesus says, "Can any one of you by worrying add a single hour to your life?" (Matthew 6:27). Here in the form of a rhetorical question Jesus is stating the obvious: If worry can't even add something as small as sixty minutes to our lives, why would you think it could help you with anything that's substantive and important? Why would you devote so much time and energy to an activity that has no possibility of improving your life in any way?

Has worry ever solved a problem or healed a hurt? Has anxiety ever created a solution, given birth to hope, calmed our hearts, or brought God's power to a desperate situation?

Prayer has. Seeking wise counsel has. Godly planning has. Reading the Scriptures has. But worry? Never. Jesus says it can't even add a single hour to our lives, much less solve the big problems of our lives.

Golfers often do the funniest thing. I can make fun of golfers since I don't play. I decided a long time ago that there are so many things I don't do well that I don't need to spend that much time or money to be bad at something else. But many golfers do the strangest thing. Pros do it. Amateurs do it. And if you've ever played golf—or even Putt Putt—you've probably done it, too. You talk to the ball.

You step up to the tee, take a swing, and when the ball starts to go wide right, you do what? You motion for the ball to go the other way with your driver or putter. You jerk your hips and wave your arms. And you yell at the ball, "Go left. Get over. Get in the hole."

Have you ever seen that work? I mean, have you ever seen a ball suddenly stop, make a ninety-degree turn to the left, drop onto the green, and then roll into the hole just because someone is performing a series of gyrations that are more awkward than me on the dance floor?

No? Then why do golfers do that? Because they are human beings, and human beings, even when we are powerless, want to be in control.

That's exactly what worry is: trying to be in control when we are powerless to change things. Worry is trying to maintain the illusion that if we just say the right thing, hold on to the problem a little longer, or fuss over it one more time, then we'll be able to create a new outcome—when, actually, we are incapable of doing so.

According to Jesus, that's just plain foolish. It's no more effective than telling a golf ball to turn left and "get in the hole." And as we're about to see, it's the very opposite of prayer.

Prescription #2: Prayer 5.20

We worry when we refuse to admit that we aren't in control. We pray when we acknowledge we're not in control and ask God to take over. Prayer is both an admission that life is bigger than we are and a declaration that God is bigger than life. Real prayer is possible only when we humble ourselves and acknowledge the biblical truth that we can't even predict what's going to happen, much less control what's going to happen. As James tells us, "Now listen, you who say, 'Today or tomorrow we will go to this or that city, spend a year there, carry on business and make money.' Why, you do not even know what will happen tomorrow. What is your life? You are a mist that appears for a little while and then vanishes" (James 4:13-14).

There is a traditional Chinese fable about a farmer who possessed an old horse that he used to plow his fields. One day the horse ran off into the hills, and the farmer's neighbors gathered around him and told him how sorry they were for his bad luck. But the farmer replied, "Bad luck or good luck? Who knows?"

A week later, the horse returned with a herd of wild horses from the hills, who followed it into the farmer's barn. This time the neighbors congratulated the farmer on his good luck. He responded, "Good luck or bad luck? Who knows?"

When the farmer's son was attempting to tame the wild horses, one of the horses fell on the young man and broke his leg. Again, the neighbors gathered to sympathize with the farmer over his bad luck. But the farmer's response was still the same: "Bad luck or good luck? Who knows?"

Some weeks later, the emperor's army marched into the village and conscripted every able-bodied youth they found there for a coming battle. When they saw the farmer's son with his broken leg, they allowed him to remain with his father.

Was that good luck or bad luck? Who knows?

The prayer that brings peace is not about "turning bad luck into good" or convincing God to give us what we think will be good for us in the moment. The prayer that leads to joy is a humble admission that we can't predict or control what's going to happen tomorrow. In fact, very often, we don't even understand what's happening in the present—whether it's going to turn out good or bad. Prayer is a confession that life is bigger than we are and that we need strength and wisdom greater than our own in order to live well.

Making that admission is not only difficult but actually offensive to many people. We do not like to admit that we are not omni-competent and that, in many ways, we are lacking in knowledge, insufficient in strength, and unprepared for what lies ahead. Many of us find it very important to our sense of self to believe we can handle life on our own. We claim we don't need anyone's help to run our lives.

Have you ever noticed how often people who claim they can handle life on their own end up just that way—on their own—because their pride and their need to control everything has alien-ated them from everyone? Have you ever noticed how often people who say prayer is nothing but a crutch use alcohol or money or success to give themselves a sense of security and self-worth? I've discovered that often those who are most wounded and broken inside are the ones who insist they can handle life on their own and refuse to acknowledge they need the help that only God can give.

But prayer—the kind of prayer that brings peace and opens the door to joy—begins when we admit life is bigger than we are and we decide to trust the One who is bigger than life. Isn't that how all recovery begins, whether it's recovery from the power of alcohol or the power of worry? We acknowledge that we have a problem, we come to believe that a higher Power can restore us to wholeness, and we consciously turn our lives over to God's care.

The prayer that acknowledges how small and powerless we are but dares to trust in the kindness and power of God has the opposite effect of worry on our lives. It removes the weight of the world from our shoulders and sets us free to do what we can do as we leave the rest to God.

In the psalms we are instructed to "Be still, and know that I am God" (Psalm 46:10). Prayer is a vacation we give ourselves from playing God and trying to fix everyone and everything. It means that, for the moment, I don't have to worry because I've decided God is in control and I'm not God.

This means that when we pray, we don't need to tell God what to do to fix things. You've heard people pray that prayer. Maybe you've prayed that prayer yourself. You tell God that you're turning your problems over, and you lay them all at his feet. But before you go, you place in God's hands your to-do list of what needs to be done, when it needs to be done, and how it needs to be done. That's not prayer. That's just worrying in the presence of God.

The prayer that brings peace and the possibility of joy asks God to change what's going on in us more than what's going on around us. If God gets us out of a crisis but doesn't get the crisis-thinking out of us, if God removes us from the chaos but doesn't remove the chaos that's in us, then in no time we'll make a mess of the good times and invent things to worry about, once again living worried and afraid.

Our hope is that God will transform us from the inside out—that God will change our hearts, strengthen our faith, and build our character. That's what we should be praying for. Then, whatever our circumstances may be, we will be able to face life with confidence and joy.

Ralph Sockman wrote, "We use prayer as a boatman uses a boat hook: to pull the boat to the shore and not to try to pull the shore to the boat."[5] The prayer that brings peace, then, is not about us changing God or convincing God to change our circumstances. The prayer that brings joy asks God to change us until we can trust him with our futures and the futures of those we love.

Description #3: Worry Leads to Defeat

Spend your time worrying about the future, and you will fail in the present. Be anxious about tomorrow, and you won't be able to handle today. Jesus put it this way: "Therefore do not worry about tomorrow, for tomorrow will worry about itself. Each day has enough trouble of its own" (Matthew 6:34).

When the Israelites were wandering in the desert, each day God provided them with just enough manna for that day with the promise that he would provide what they needed for the next day when the new day arrived—but not before then. God was trying to teach them a lesson: "Depend on me one day at a time, and I will nourish you and give you what you need one day at a time."

God wants to teach us the same lesson, because that's still the way he works. He gives us the strength we need to face our problems one day at a time. That means he will give us the energy and the insight we need for today, today.

"Each day has enough trouble of its own." When we allow ourselves to worry about the future, we give today's strength to tomorrow's fears. That means we won't have the strength we need to do what today calls for—not because God hasn't given us what we need, but because we have wasted what he has given. As a result, we will find ourselves drained, depressed, and defeated. A quotation attributed to Charles Spurgeon reminds us, "Anxiety does not empty tomorrow of its sorrow, but only empties today of its strength."[6] God will give us what we need for each day. We must not give that strength to tomorrow. If we do, we will fail today.

Sometimes it seems we have too much to carry. We feel weak and overwhelmed. In her book *Finding Water: The Art of Perseverance*, Julia Cameron writes: "'God does not give us more than we can handle,' I am told but I wonder if God doesn't overestimate me just a little."[7] We've all been there. We all have felt that life was more than we could bear. That maybe God was "overestimating us." But the promise of God is, "My grace is sufficient for you, for my power is made perfect in weakness" (2 Corinthians 12:9). God will give you the grace you need, but he will give it to you one day at a time. Don't waste the grace and the strength that God provides you for today by worrying about things that might not even happen tomorrow.

Robert Hastings says it so well: "It isn't the burdens of today that drive men mad. It is the regrets over yesterday and the fear of tomorrow."[8] Regret and worry are twin thieves that rob us of strength and joy today.

Through the years, I have watched many people destroy themselves because they wouldn't stop worrying about tomorrow, often about things that never happened. And I have witnessed the enormous strength that people who trust in God possess, which enables them to face great burdens and overcome terrible tragedies as they address them one day at a time.

Prescription #3: Do Today What You Can Do and Leave the Rest to God

Sir William Osler, the famous physician and one of the four founders of Johns Hopkins University, is sometimes referred to as the father of modern medicine. He wrote about a time when he was consumed with anxiety. It was shortly before his final exams, and his mind was wracked with concerns about the exam and his future career. Pacing around his room, he spotted on a shelf a copy of a book written by the Scottish author and historian Thomas Carlyle. As he began to read, he came upon this sentence: "Our main business is not to see what lies dimly at a distance, but to do what lies clearly at hand."[9] Years later while addressing students at Yale, Dr. Osler described how Carlyle's insight had helped him that evening and how it had been foundational for all his future successes. He told the young people gathered before him, no doubt concerned about their own futures, that Carlyle's advice to settle down to the day's work and let the future take care of itself "hit and stuck and helped, and was the starting-point of a habit that has enabled me to utilize to the full the single talent entrusted to me."[10]

People who are free from anxiety are not people who are free of problems or who can see how the future will turn out. They are people who make decisions and act. They determine what they can do today—what "lies at hand," in the words of Thomas Carlyle— and they do it now.

If prayer is needed, they pray. If speaking to someone is needed, they speak. If gaining more information about a problem is needed, they learn more about what they are facing. If silence is needed, they are silent. If action is needed, they act. If waiting patiently is needed, they wait until it's the right time to proceed. They do what today's trouble calls for and leave the rest to God. The miracle is that when we do what we can do, God steps in and does the rest in ways we could never imagine.

Sadly, I have met with many couples who have a child who is abusing or is addicted to drugs. Like my close friend I mentioned at the beginning of this chapter, they are confused, frightened, and in paralyzing pain. After listening to them, I ask them to determine what they can do right now. What's the next step they can take that will be helpful? Then we make a plan for them to do that.

But before they leave, I tell them, "You cannot let this problem consume you." I have children myself. I know how much these parents love their child and how fearful they are for him or her. But I also know that if they are consumed with fear, they will not make good decisions for that child, they likely will not be present for the needs of their other children (if they have them) or other family members, and their relationships with one another will suffer. It's so common that when a child is addicted to drugs or severely ill or in some other kind of danger that the parents find themselves angry and upset with each other. At the very time when it's most important that they come together, their anxiety causes them to pull apart, blame each other for their child's problems, and become angry that their spouse has different ideas about how to handle the problem.

I always tell these parents, "This is a huge problem. It's a big part of your life, but it's only a part of your life. Do what you can do about it today and then emotionally step away from it. Do something together that you enjoy. Spend time with your other children or loved ones. Exercise regularly. Enjoy your hobby."

Some parents can't do that. They think if they're not worrying constantly about their child, it's a sign that they don't care, that they're not doing their job. I try to impress on them that they should do these things so that they can "do their job" of caring for their child who's in trouble.

If you want to help a child or loved one, then you need to stay healthy physically, emotionally, and spiritually. And if you're married, you will help your child or loved one best if your marriage stays strong, with the two of you working together. Yes, you'll have different ideas about what's best, and there will be conflict. That's why you need to do all you can to spend the time and do the things that will deepen your relationship and bring you closer to each other. It seems counterintuitive. But when you have the most to worry about, that's when you need to worry least and focus on what makes you and your other relationships healthy and strong.

How do you do that? Determine what you can do today to learn what you need to learn, decide what you need to decide, and do what you need to do. Write it down, even. Then do it. And once you've done that, give yourself permission—if need be, force yourself—to let it go and leave the rest to God.

Tomorrow, there may be more to learn, decide, and do. But once you've done what you can do today, let it go and do something positive and healthy with the rest of your day. This takes practice and discipline. You'll probably catch yourself falling back into worry even after you've said, "I've done all I can for today." But you can make progress and worry a little less every day. And eventually you will get to a place where, with God's help, you can let each day worry about itself.

When it comes to determining "what you can do today" to manage your stress, there are better ways of coping than the common habits of drinking, taking drugs, overeating, shopping, or zoning out in front of a television or a computer screen. We have already considered how vital prayer and reading God's word are. Let's look at a few other beneficial habits.

Memorize and contemplate God's promises. Either your circumstances or God's promises will determine your inner state—whether you live anxiously or with joy. So, memorize, contemplate, and claim God's promises—such as "I know the plans I have for you, . . . plans to prosper you and not to harm you" (Jeremiah 29:11); "My grace is sufficient for you" (2 Corinthians 12:9); and "I am with you always, to the very end of the age" (Matthew 28:20). When you find yourself becoming anxious, repeat these promises to yourself slowly, taking them into your spirit and letting them calm your soul.

Talk to someone about your problems. Burdens always become lighter when they are shared. The Christian life is not a solo project. You'll help someone at another time when they need a listening ear. Let someone—a friend you trust, a pastor or a counselor—help you now.

Exercise. Go for a walk each day. Attend a class at a nearby gym or your church. Lift weights. Find a sport or active hobby you enjoy. Even better, do so with a friend. The mind-body connection is biblical. It's how God made us. A healthy body will help you level out emotionally.

Help someone else. When you're tired and feeling overwhelmed, it's hard to think about serving others; but it's one of the best ways to handle your stress.

Karl Menninger, arguably the greatest psychiatrist of the twentieth century, was once asked what treatment he would recommend for someone who was anxious and depressed. To the surprise of his audience, he said that he would tell that person to leave their house, go to the other side of the tracks, find someone who was worse off, and help that person.

One of the great truths that Jesus taught is that we find life when we give ourselves away. Serving others puts our problems in perspective and makes us feel good about ourselves. Even if it's in a way that's small, find a way to serve others. Take a meal to an elderly neighbor. Work in the local food bank. Help build a Habitat for Humanity home. If your church provides rides for the elderly or supports a shelter or has a visitation ministry to persons who are homebound, get involved—even if it's just once a week for a couple of hours. Getting our eyes off of ourselves, caring for someone else, and feeling productive is immensely helpful in lifting our spirits and bringing joy.

If you've gotten into a bad pattern of how you handle your stress, change your pattern to something healthy. Change it today.

One of our great American poets was Sidney Lanier. All his life he loved the outdoors, and much of his poetry expresses the joy he received from being in the rugged, beautiful world that God created. When he was nineteen, the Civil War began. Lanier fought, was captured, and contracted tuberculosis in prison. Shortly after the war, he married and had four children.

As his condition worsened, he knew he would not live long (tuberculosis was always fatal then). He travelled to Glynn County on the Georgia Coast where the climate was milder. We can only imagine the worry and the fear that must have filled his heart as he contemplated his life—what was before him and what would become of his family. It was at this time that he wrote his finest poem, "The Marshes of Glynn," which tells of a day spent observing the massive watery marshes that separate the coastal islands of Glynn County from the Georgia mainland. As he describes walking to the coast and passing through thick woods and underbrush, he uses these images to represent the harshness and the uncertainties and the unfairness of life.

But then as he contemplates "the length and the breadth" of the marshes of Glynn, everything changes for him. He writes, "Somehow my soul seems suddenly free."[11] What is it that has set him free from the fear and the burden of what fate has brought to him? These lines give us the answer:

> As the marsh-hen secretly builds on the watery sod,
> Behold I will build me a nest on the greatness of God:
> I will fly in the greatness of God as the marsh-hen flies
> In the freedom that fills all the space 'twixt the marsh
> and the skies:

By so many roots as the marsh-grass sends in the sod
I will heartily lay me a-hold on the greatness of God:
Oh, like to the greatness of God is the greatness within
The range of the marshes, the liberal marshes of Glynn.[12]

When he felt overwhelmed and anxious, an awareness of the greatness of God set him free. The poet remembers the vastness and the depth and the strength and the goodness of God, and he decides that God can be trusted.

There's that word again: *decide*. Choose. You don't have to be afraid. You do not have to live anxious and worried. You do not have to carry the weight or fight the battle by yourself. God is still God; and whatever your problem is, God is greater.

Earlier I quoted Julia Cameron, saying, " 'God does not give us more than we can handle,' I am told but I wonder if God doesn't overestimate me just a little." Here's how she finishes that thought: "Or perhaps, and this is likely, I underestimate God."[13]

You have a great God whose power is infinite and whose wisdom is beyond your imagining. He loves with a love that will not let you go. Don't underestimate him. Build your nest on the greatness of God, not on the uncertainties of life that cause you to worry and fear.

Choose to do what you can do today. Then decide to trust God and leave the rest to him.

2

BITTERNESS

"In your anger do not sin": Do not let the sun go down while you are still angry, and do not give the devil a foothold. . . . Get rid of all bitterness, rage and anger, brawling and slander, along with every form of malice. Be kind and compassionate to one another, forgiving each other, just as in Christ God forgave you.

(Ephesians 4:26-27, 31-32)

It will sap your strength and rob your joy. It has the power to poison your relationships with others. Unchecked it can harden your heart toward God. In fact, it can destroy your soul.

It's called *bitterness*. It's more than the flash of anger we feel when we have been hurt deeply and unfairly. It's the anger we have held on to until it has gained the power to hold on to us. It's an old wound that has never healed, but instead, has become infected and inflamed. At times, it may feel like a raging fire, burning deep inside our souls as we remember the wrong we suffered. At other times, it's the pain within our hearts which, once warm and tender, are becoming cold and hard. Either way, anger allowed to linger will turn into bitterness, and bitterness will steal our joy.

Some of you may be tempted to skip this chapter. You may be thinking anger and bitterness are topics that don't apply to you. There are two possible reasons you may feel that way. The first is that you have already done the hard work of forgiving everyone who has ever hurt you. The second is that you're in denial about what happened to you and the person(s) you need to forgive. You have buried your hurt so deeply that you're not consciously aware of it any longer. Or you know that it's there, but looking at it honestly is so threatening to you, that you have decided to ignore it.

Isn't there a third option? Isn't it possible that you don't really have anyone to forgive? Yes, that's possible—in some kind of alternative, imaginary universe that doesn't actually exist.

In the real world, we hurt others and others hurt us. Our selfishness brings pain to other people, and the selfishness of other people brings pain into our lives. When the pain we experience is deep and unfair, there is no real cure other than forgiveness.

One of the joys of being a pastor is being involved in the most real and important moments in the lives of people. We are given the gift of sharing in their happiness—events like weddings, births, and baptisms. But we are also invited to share the most painful times in the lives of people—the loss of a spouse, illness, job loss, the death of a child, moral failures, broken marriages, and betrayal.

When I talk with men and women who are honest with me, I find there is pain in their lives. All of us carry some burden that makes life difficult. We bear the pain of something we have done, and we suffer because of something that was done to us. Maybe we grew up with a parent who was overly critical and demeaning, even abusive. And though he or she may live far away or no longer be living at all, their words still have a crippling effect on our life and how we feel about ourselves. It could be a business partner who cheated us. A spouse who betrayed us. A child who rejected our love and walked out of our lives. Or someone we hardly know who spread vicious rumors about us. A senseless act of violence or carelessness has left us disabled forever.

For many of us, the burden isn't what someone did. It's what someone didn't do. You may have grown up with a father or a mother who was never there for you, physically or emotionally. If so, you suffered a wound of absence. Though it didn't leave a mark on your body, it left a hole in your heart. Maybe a friend or an older sibling failed to defend you when you were attacked verbally or physically, and you have felt alone ever since. It could be that a pastor or your church wasn't supportive when you were struggling and needed their love and help. Some of our deepest wounds are not the results of what was done to us, but they come from the times that someone we thought we could count on didn't do anything at all. None of us goes through this world without getting hurt and hurt deeply. If we don't deal with our wounds honestly, whether we know it or not, they remains inside us. Even if it happened long ago, even if it was when we were children, the effects of what was done to us are still there, either raging like a white-hot fire or quietly turning our souls into ice.

Don't deal with your pain, don't forgive, let your wound turn into bitterness, and it will steal your joy and spill over into the other areas of your life. It will not only harm you, but it will eventually injure the people you love.

The writer of Hebrews warns us: "Make every effort to live in peace with everyone and to be holy; without holiness no one will see the Lord. See to it that no one falls short of the grace of God and that no bitter root grows up to cause trouble and defile many" (Hebrews 12:14-15).

What's the result when we don't allow the grace of God to remove our anger and heal our wounds? A root of bitterness is planted within our hearts. And our bitterness creates an angry spirit that brings trouble and dysfunction into the lives of others who often don't deserve it.

"Do You Want to Be Whole?"

If bitterness is so painful for us to bear and so dangerous to those around us, why would anyone hold on to it? There are many reasons. One reason is that, like anything we feed, bitterness gets bigger and stronger over time. Any attitude or habit we indulge over time grows more and more powerful. When we allow anger to remain in our spirits, it becomes a stronghold that imprisons us. In Ephesians 4 it is described as "a foothold" for the devil. In other words, when we hold on to anger, we give it the power to hold on to us. Strongholds are not easily broken, and they do not surrender their hold on us without a struggle. Like the unclean spirits that often put up a fight when Jesus commanded them to come out of a tormented soul, bitterness will not release us from its grip simply because we finally see the damage it's doing in our lives and we wish it would leave. Our freedom will necessitate a spiritual battle.

Another reason people don't let go of their bitterness is because in a way that is twisted and perverse, anger can be enjoyable. Frederick Buechner wrote, "Of the Seven Deadly Sins, anger is possibly the most fun. To lick your wounds, to smack your lips over grievances long past, to roll over your tongue the prospect of bitter confrontations still to come, to savor to the last toothsome morsel both the pain you are given and the pain you are giving back—in many ways it is a feast fit for a king. The chief drawback is that what you are wolfing down is yourself. The skeleton at the feast is you."[1]

Why do people feast day after day on a fast-food diet they know is unhealthy? Because it tastes good. In fact, the fat content and the amount of salt in many fast-food dishes have been purposefully and carefully engineered to produce an almost addictive reaction within the consumer. Even as people hate themselves for downing another high calorie, grease-laden meal, they feel the familiar comfort of a taste they have come to love.

Bitterness can be the same way. We know that it is unhealthy. But at the same time, it brings the pleasurable feelings of righteous indignation, moral superiority, and the dream of one day getting even.

Still another reason why people don't forgive and let go of their bitterness is this: They are afraid. Some people don't know who they will be without their anger, because their identity is so enmeshed with being a victim. The wrong done to them has provided an excuse for their not moving forward in life. If they forgive, they will have to change how they live and who they are. And they fear that the devil they don't know—a new identity and a new way of living—might be worse than the bitter devil they do know.

Teresa grew up in a dysfunctional family. Her father was mentally and physically abusive. He was an executive in a large company, and he treated his children the way he treated his firm's low-level employees. He gave the orders, and they were expected to fulfill them. Period.

Teresa's mother had checked out emotionally. She avoided her husband's abuse through her depression and imaginary illnesses that caused her to spend most of her time in bed. Teresa served as the surrogate mother for her siblings. As is typical in dysfunctional families, one member, in this instance Teresa, did everything for everybody and at the same time was made to feel inadequate and unworthy of love and respect. She was constantly given the message she had never done enough to be proud of herself, much less believe that she was smart or kind or pretty, all of which she was.

We met several times. At our first meeting, it was apparent that Teresa understood how her father had abused her, and she was angry that he had never appreciated her, never thanked her, never loved her. But she felt guilty for hating him. I helped her understand that being angry about how she had been treated was not wrong. I did my best to impress on her that she was a child of God who deserved not only to be loved for who she was but to be praised for all she had done for her siblings. But I knew that she would never be whole unless she could forgive her father. It was fine for her to be angry with him, but she would be free from her past only if she could overcome her bitterness toward him.

We looked together at Jesus' encounter with the man beside the pool who had been paralyzed for thirty-eight years and who was bitter about how others had ignored his needs and taken care of themselves. We read how Jesus asked him what appears to be the strangest question in the entire Bible, "Do you want to get well?" (John 5:6). Another way to translate that question is, "Do you want to be whole?" I sent her home with the assignment not to forgive her father, but to list all that would have to change if she forgave her father and God made her whole.

Dutiful and wanting to please, she took the task very seriously. The next week she returned with several pages of notes.

"If God made me whole," she wrote, "I could no longer use my childhood as a reason for feeling so bad. I would have to be responsible for how I feel. I'd have to quit doing everything for everybody. I'd have to learn to say no. If God made me whole, I'd have to love myself and take care of myself. I'd have to let others love me even when I didn't feel like I deserved to be loved. I'd have to quit hiding the real me from my friends. I'd have to quit hating my father." The list went on and on. Finally, she looked up and said, "My whole life, my whole world would have to change."

My eyes met hers. I said softly, "Teresa, God can give you the grace to forgive. He can heal you. Do you want to be whole?"

When you understand the full ramifications of forgiving the person who harmed you, how your life might change, how you would have to let go of your crutches and your excuses, how your future might become more challenging, not less, and how you might have to love yourself and give yourself permission to experience real joy, it can be frightening. And some of us choose to hold on to the bitterness that traps us in a life that is painful but familiar.

How about you? Do you want to be whole? Are you willing to stop blaming others for how you feel or where you are in life? Are you willing to be set free from the delicious taste and addictive power of bitterness so you can experience a life of freedom and joy? If so, forgiveness is your way out. It's your way forward. It's the only way.

Here's my definition of forgiveness: Forgiveness is a process by which we separate the person who hurt us from the action that hurt us and bring healing to ourselves. More on the process in just a moment.

First, I want to stress that forgiveness brings about a separation. In our minds and in our hearts, forgiveness separates the person who hurt us from the action that hurt us.

In the New Testament, the Greek word often translated into English as "to forgive" is *aphiēmi*. But it can be translated by many other English words as well. See if you can recognize the common thought behind all of these definitions.

Aphiēmi can mean "to hurl" an object, such as a rock or a spear. It can mean "to depart from" a place, "to set aside" a commandment, or "to leave behind" someone or something. It can also mean "to divorce."[2]

Do you see what's similar in all these different meanings for *aphiēmi*? In each case, there is the idea of separation. Distance is created between two persons or two objects, whether that distance is physical, emotional, or legal.

That's what we do when we forgive someone who hurt us. In the way we relate to the other person, we put distance between that person and what he or she did to us.

Look how beautifully this is expressed in the Psalms.

> *He does not treat us as our sins deserve*
> *or repay us according to our iniquities. . . .*
> *As far as the east is from the west,*
> *so far has he removed our transgressions from us.*
> (Psalm 103:10, 12)

Forgiveness is a process of separation. In our hearts, we remove a person's sins from who he or she is so we can relate to that person differently. In our minds, we may still remember what the person did to us, but how we feel and act is no longer controlled by the harm we experienced. And in the process, we are freed from the spiritual poison of anger and bitterness.

If you've been hurt deeply that may sound crazy, in fact, impossible. You may not want to forgive. You may want to scream through these pages at me, "Rob, you don't know what you're asking me to do. You don't know what he did to me." You're right.

But I do know what you're doing to yourself. I know that bitterness doesn't harm the person who hurt you; it only deepens your own pain. And over time it will destroy you.

Even if you want to forgive—if your wound is deep—it's not easy. There is no reset button you can push so that all the pain immediately goes away. You can't just decide not to be angry anymore. But you can decide to begin the process that will free you from anger, the process of forgiving.

Before we discuss the steps to forgiveness, let me say that not all hurts need to be forgiven. Life is full of slights, annoyances, and little acts of meanness. These don't need to be forgiven. They need to be shrugged off and forgotten.

I made up a saying that helps me keep little things little. "It takes more than one jerk to ruin my day." I don't have to let the little things somebody does that irritate me consume my thoughts or linger in my spirit. Most of the time, I can just let them go and move on.

But there are times when not only is shrugging off our pain not possible, it's unhealthy. That's when the pain is deep and the harm is significant, whether the damage is physical, emotional, financial, or relational. Acting like real harm is no big deal is not a sign of spiritual maturity or strength of character. It's evidence that either we are uncomfortable with conflict or we don't believe we are worthy of respect and joy.

How do we move into the process of forgiveness? Let's consider three steps.

1. We must "have" our pain.

I know that's a strange statement, but what I mean is that we must feel the injustice we have suffered and acknowledge the pain that our wound has caused us.

Some people never forgive because they don't allow themselves to hurt. There are all kinds of reasons why we may refuse to feel our pain.

We may think it's a sign of weakness to hurt. I grew up playing a game called, "That doesn't hurt." My brother or an older boy would knuckle-punch me in the arm as hard as he could, and immediately I'd say, "That doesn't hurt." He'd keep hitting me, and I'd keep saying, "That doesn't hurt." There would be tears in my eyes, my arm would feel like it was falling off, and I'd be praying for the immediate return of Jesus. But my response never changed. Why? Because I didn't want to give the other guy the satisfaction of knowing that he had hurt me. In my mind, if I denied my pain, I would win, and he would lose.

Some of us learn to play that game with our emotional wounds because we think it's weak to admit pain. Maybe an abusive parent made fun of us for crying after we were scolded or whipped. Or the other kids laughed at us when they saw that our feelings had been hurt. It could be a spouse who mocks us when it's apparent that we have been wounded by his or her critical attacks.

As a defense, we decide that not only will we never let anyone see us hurting; we won't feel pain at all. We won't give another person the satisfaction of knowing that she or he hurt us. And we promise ourselves that we'll never again be weak enough to let anyone get to us. We turn off our feelings because we hate feeling weak. When we do that, we die a bit inside. And we end up hating a part of ourselves because all of us are weak enough to bleed when we are wounded, even if it's "only" cutting words or a stab in the back that has injured us.

Others of us may not admit our pain because we're afraid we may end up hating the person we need most. If we acknowledge what someone did to us, we may have to admit that the other person doesn't love us as deeply as we wish—or at all. Or we fear if we get angry with him or her, the person will ll leave us, and we'll be alone.

There's another reason we don't allow ourselves to hurt. That's because it hurts to hurt. It is painful to remember what was done to us—the fear we felt; the excruciating agony of being betrayed by someone we thought we could depend upon; how lost and alone we felt because a parent loved alcohol more than they loved us; how deeply we suffered when we appeared small and inadequate in front of our peers because of the words or the actions of another child. So we ignore our pain. We push it out of our minds. We act like it never happened.

What is the result? We never forgive; we never get healed; we never become whole. Our hearts become hard, and we live disconnected from our souls.

Please, hear this. You cannot give to God what you do not have. That's why the first step in forgiving another person is having our pain. We become honest about what was done to us. We don't minimize the damage we suffered or the pain we endured. And we take the risk of feeling our feelings, not to wallow in them, but so we can give them to God and be set free from the power of the past.

The film *Antwone Fisher* is a true story about a young man who grew up in an abusive foster home. Over the years, Fisher grew bitter toward his natural family for giving him up. By the time he enlisted in the Navy, his anger had gotten him into so many fights that he was sent to a Naval psychologist, Dr. Jerome Davenport. After they have built a relationship of caring and trust, Fisher spends Thanksgiving with the psychologist's family.

When the dinner is over, Fisher reads a poem, which he had written. The poem repeats a single question over and over throughout: "Who will cry for the little boy?" Fisher's poem describes the pain of his childhood—the loneliness, abandonment, rejection, lack of love or a sense of belonging. Finally, the poem ends with the question, "Who will cry for the little boy? Who cries inside of me?"[3]

When he finishes reading, Dr. Davenport asks, "Who will cry for the little boy, Antwone?" Fisher responds, "I will."

Today Antwone Fisher is a successful screenwriter, poet, and best-selling author. His healing from the anger and bitterness that were destroying his life began as he became honest and courageous enough to feel the hurt he had suffered, cry for what he had lost, and "have his pain." Until you have your pain, it will have you. It may show up as anger or as an addiction or as depression or as feeling dead inside. But it will have you.

If you want to be healed, you must give your pain to God so he can take it from you. But first, you must acknowledge what was done to you and feel the loss you suffered. It may mean crying for the little boy or the little girl who cries inside of you. This work is often best done with a counselor who will encourage you to push deeper until you have all the pain that resides within your wound—and who will support you as you do this difficult and courageous spiritual work.

Once we have our pain, we are ready for the next step.

2. We must hold the person(s) who harmed us responsible for their actions.

Some of us have a hard time forgiving because we don't want to let go of our anger. But others of us find forgiveness difficult because we don't want to hold others responsible for their actions. We are willing to make excuses for the person who hurt us. But excusing is not the same as forgiving. What's the difference?

Excusing says someone is not responsible for what she or he did. Forgiveness says she or he is.

What makes us different from other species is that we are morally accountable for our actions. We are made in the image of God. We possess a conscience. We can choose good over evil. And we are responsible for the choices we make. This moral accountability is one of the traits that distinguishes us from other creatures—it's a huge part of what makes us human. So when one person excuses another's bad behavior and denies his responsibility for his actions, though it may seem like a gracious act, it's just the opposite. It denies the other person his or her humanity.

We excuse someone when we say things like, "My boyfriend doesn't really mean to hurt me. He just gets so mad he can't control himself." "My mother did her best. She just couldn't be there for me because she was an alcoholic." "My father demeaned every dream I ever had, but that's how he was raised." "My wife cheated on me, but I wasn't giving her the emotional support she needed."

These words sound gracious and kind, but they are the opposite. Understanding why someone did something may make forgiveness easier. But denying that others are responsible for what they did denies their humanity and their ability to change. There is nothing kind or compassionate in that.

The problem for some of us may be that if we hold people responsible for what they did, we're afraid we may become angry with them. Indeed, we may. And very often we should. Anger in the face of evil is a proper response. Even when the evil is done to us.

Jesus became angry when he saw the poor and the suffering mistreated in the name of religion (Mark 3:4-6). He became angry when he witnessed hypocrisy (Matthew 23:13-32). He became angry enough to make a whip and turn over the money changers' tables when he saw that their greed was hurting people (John 2:13-17). If Jesus was angry on numerous occasions, then anger isn't necessarily wrong. In fact, it can be a very righteous response.

We do need to be careful with our anger. You've probably heard it said that "anger" is one letter away from "danger." Aristotle taught that anger can be an appropriate response and that not being angry at times is a deficiency in character. But he went on to say "it is not easy to determine what is the right way to be angry, and with whom, and on what grounds, and for how long."[4] In other words, making sure we are angry at the right person, to the right degree and for the right reason and for no longer than we should be—that's hard.

But just because it's hard to do anger the right way doesn't mean that anger itself is necessarily wrong. When Paul writes about getting rid of bitterness and malice and forgiving one another in Ephesians 4, he begins by writing, "In your anger do not sin" (verse 26). It's clear here that anger is not sin. It's what we do with our anger that is right or wrong.

Becoming vengeful, striking out to harm another person—that's sinful. But admitting and feeling our anger, when we have been harmed deeply and unfairly, is right and healthy.

I grew up in Texas City, Texas, on the Gulf Coast. Blessed with a natural deep-water harbor, it's home to several oil refineries, chemical plants and, when I was a boy, the only tin smelter in the United States. When I brought friends home from college, they all said the same thing. "Renfroe, this is the ugliest, smelliest place I've ever seen." Cites have mottoes. "Gateway to the West" (St. Louis). "The City That Never Sleeps" (New York). "The Biggest Little City in the World" (Reno). Texas City doesn't have a motto, but a good one would be "On a Clear Day You Must Be Somewhere Else."

Texas City was one of the EPA's Superfund cleanup sites. Radioactive and toxic materials were found under the soil. Why not just leave them there? They were out of sight. Truth is, people weren't even aware those deadly chemicals were there. Why not just let them be? Because toxic chemicals make people sick. Just because you're not aware of something nearby that's poisonous and unhealthy, it doesn't mean that it's not affecting you.

When we excuse someone who has harmed us, all we are doing is pushing our anger so far down into our subconscious that we think we've gotten rid of it. But that doesn't mean it's gone away. Like toxic waste plowed under and covered up, it's still there poisoning and contaminating our lives.

I went to seminary outside of Boston, Massachusetts, in a small idyllic New England town. For our second year, my wife, Peggy, and I signed up for the inner-city program. We lived in a poor white working-class neighborhood in the city where the unemployment rate was 25 percent.

The teenagers there came to hate us. We were clearly outsiders. Our Texas accents and my long hair marked us as different right off. But the main reason the teenagers had a problem with us is that we were open in our belief that the black kids who lived three blocks away should be able to play in the neighborhood park just the same as the white kids.

We had an interesting year. Half the time I stepped out of the house, someone would call me an offensive name meant to demean me by questioning my sexuality. The rest of the time I was addressed with another derisive term, just as bad in their eyes, "Hey, liberal."

This was a difficult time in Boston's history when white kids were being bused to schools in black neighborhoods and black children were being bused into white communities. There were national news stories about white parents throwing bricks and rocks at buses with black children inside them going to school. The families where we lived knew how wrong we thought this kind of prejudice was.

The teenagers in our neighborhood stole our car twice. They threatened to burn down our house because we brought a young black woman home from the church we attended for lunch. Once they dug up a dead cat and smeared it on our door.

I thought I was handling the situation pretty well. I was a Christian, a soon-to-be minister. And I knew Jesus had told me to love my enemies. So, I smiled. I said "hello" politely no matter how I was accosted. I ignored their insults.

Imagine my surprise one night when I woke up from a dream in which I had met a dozen of those teenagers in the middle of the park and had beaten the living daylights out of them. I have to tell you that my fist smashing into their faces felt so good that when I woke up and realized I had been dreaming, I wanted to cry. The dream showed me how angry I was at those teenagers, despite my attempts to cover it up.

Did I have a right to my anger? Absolutely. Anger is a proper emotion in the face of something that's wrong. Even if the wrong is being done to you.

But here's the problem. If we don't deal with our anger honestly, just push it down deep into our subconscious and ignore it, it will go underground, turn into bitterness, and fester within our souls. I had buried my toxic anger toward those teenagers underground in my subconscious, but it was there—poisoning my spirit and disturbing my dreams.

Do you get upset with people easily? Is there an underlying spirit of anger within you? Are you depressed when you have many reasons to be happy? Are you suspicious of people and defensive when you don't need to be? Are you guarded with what you let others know about yourself? Do you find yourself wondering why you're not living with joy when you consider all the blessings that should make you grateful?

The reason could be that there is unresolved anger in your life about harm that you have suffered. That anger will dwell within you and lash out in inappropriate ways at people who don't deserve it. Or you'll have to expend so much psychological energy to push it down into your subconscious and keep it buried that you will be emotionally drained and unable to experience the joy God desires for you.

When we are angry, the solution is never to act like our anger doesn't exist. The right response is to admit that it's there and to feel it. That doesn't happen if we make excuses for the person who hurt us and fail to hold him or her responsible for the damage they've done.

Fail to do the work, short-change the process, deny your anger, and you'll be great at suppression. But you'll be terrible at forgiving.

The Book of Hebrews talks about a root of bitterness. Until we have our pain, hold responsible the person who created it, and allow ourselves to be angry, we'll never get to the root of the issue. We'll just be clipping off the top of the weeds that are growing from the bottom of our hearts.

I thought often about the teenagers who were making our lives so miserable when we were in Boston. Many of their fathers were unemployed. Money was tight. The streets were tough. Their futures were far from bright. They had been taught to look down on other races by their parents. I did my best to empathize with where they were coming from. In a way, I could understand why they were prejudiced and why they felt a need to threaten Peggy and me. And understanding how difficult their lives were did help me process my anger and forgive them. But it didn't excuse their racism or their abusing us. They are as accountable for their actions as you and I are for ours.

Holding someone responsible for their actions and for the harm they did to us doesn't mean we are going to take them to court, exact revenge, or even demand an apology. But neither are we going to make excuses for their actions or act as if their choices are of little consequence.

Actions that don't matter don't hurt us or fracture relationships or lead to bitterness. Actions that do cannot be excused or minimized or ignored. They must be forgiven.

3. We must give our pain and anger to God, and then we are set free.

In *Shame and Grace: Healing the Shame We Don't Deserve*, Lewis Smedes writes, "When we genuinely forgive, we set a prisoner free and then discover that the prisoner we set free was us."[5]

Forgiveness is a change in us. It doesn't necessarily change the person who caused our pain. But it brings healing and wholeness to the place where we have been wounded. It sets our spirit free so we can return to life, open to receive the many blessings God has for us, including joy.

The beauty of forgiveness is that it is not dependent upon the other person. We can forgive whether the person who hurt us apologizes or not. We can forgive if the other person admits what he or she did or denies it altogether. We can forgive and be set free even if the wrong done to us is never made right.

Forgiveness is not about getting justice. The person who hurt you owes you something. An explanation. An apology. An attempt to restore your reputation. Monetary damages. A new start in life. Something.

Forgiveness lets him go. Emotionally and spiritually, you let him go. You no longer expect or demand payment. In your heart and mind this person no longer owes you anything, not because she's paid a price, but because you have cancelled the debt.

Forgiveness is not justice; it is grace. You give grace to the person who harmed you. And in your heart and mind, it's over. You are able to wish the person who hurt you well. You are healed.

On July 4, 2011, Lydia Tillman was sexually assaulted and strangled by Travis Forbes, a man she had never met. Forbes beat her head in, shattered her jaw, and left her for dead. To cover his crime, he poured bleach on her body and set her apartment on fire. Miraculously she survived, only to suffer a stroke that left her in a coma for five weeks. Many months of rehab followed, including learning how to speak again.

She describes going to court to see her attacker plead guilty and be sentenced as "the hardest day of my life." She addressed Forbes in the courtroom with three sentences which took her an hour to articulate. Her last sentence to the man who tried to kill her was, "May you find peace in this life."[6]

Still struggling with her speech, she told NBC correspondent Keith Morrison "to forgive him [Forbes] was super difficult." When Morrison asked her how she was able to do that, she said that she chose "to heal myself rather than being angry."

The interview concludes with Tillman saying, "I believe Travis Forbes was acting out of fear and hatred. I choose love and peace over fear and I win."

When you have been harmed, you deserve justice. But you can receive justice and still be bitter. The person who hurt you can apologize, and you can still be filled with rage. You can be compensated for your loss and continue to be in bondage to your pain. You only win when you forgive.

How do we experience the freedom and the healing of forgiveness? As with most miracles, God does the work, but we must do something to receive it. I have found six steps to be helpful.

1. Focus on the forgiveness God gave you. In the Ephesians 4 passage on overcoming anger and bitterness we are told, "Be kind and compassionate to one another, forgiving each other, just as in Christ God forgave you" (verse 32).

This one sentence is so rich. First, it tells us that we should forgive because God forgave us. Were it not for Christ, we would stand before God deserving judgment and condemnation. On our own we are unable to atone for our sins or repay the debt we owe. Still, God in Christ forgave us of our sins. The goal of the Christian life is to become more like Jesus—to think, love, live, and treat others the way he did. If he forgave those who sinned against him, even praying for those who nailed him to the cross, then we should strive to forgive those who hurt us.

This verse speaks clearly to those of us who struggle to forgive because the person who hurt us "doesn't deserve to be forgiven." Paul reminds us that neither do we. We were guilty and unworthy of God's mercy, but God was "kind and compassionate" to us. If the only One who is truly holy and righteous can forgive those who sinned against him, who are we sinners to withhold grace from others? Forgiving is not what we do because someone deserves to be forgiven. It's what we do to be like our Father, kind and compassionate.

Why do we forgive? Because we want to be like Christ. Because we are aware of our sins and our need for forgiveness. Because we have experienced the grace of God that humbles our pride, softens our hearts, and makes us compassionate for others who need grace.

Before you ask God to help you forgive the person who hurt you, remember the kindness that God has shown you. Remember your guilt and how you have received more than what you have deserved. Remember what it felt like to be forgiven. How surprising it was that God loved you so deeply. How grateful you were for his compassion. How you wanted to live a life that pleased him and that brought kindness and goodness into the lives of others.

Spend some time here. Remember what God has done for you, recalling the forgiveness you, a sinner, received from him.

2. *Tell God about your pain.* If you have never done so, write down the harm you suffered. List in detail all you have lost, how much you were hurt, and the parts of your life that you may never get back.

Unburden your heart. Tell God everything. Turn these notes into a prayer. Like the psalmist who told God in graphic detail about the injustice he suffered and the pain and the anger he felt, speak openly with God.

> *Ruthless witnesses come forward;*
>> *they question me on things I know nothing about.*
> *They repay me evil for good*
>> *and leave me like one bereaved.*
> *Yet when they were ill, I put on sackcloth*
>> *and humbled myself with fasting. . . .*
> *But when I stumbled, they gathered in glee;*
>> *assailants gathered against me without my knowledge.*
> *They slandered me without ceasing.*
> *Like the ungodly they maliciously mocked;*
>> *they gnashed their teeth at me.*
>>>>>>> *(Psalm 35:11-13, 15-16)*

Be honest about all you have felt. If you have wanted the person who hurt you to suffer, be honest with God about it. If you have fantasized about getting back at the other person, tell God what you have envisioned. This is a time to be real and raw. God can handle it.

3. Give up your claim on the other person. Tell God and yourself, "I no longer expect an explanation from the person who hurt me. I no longer demand an apology or satisfaction. I don't need him to admit that I was right and he was wrong. I want nothing from the person who hurt me."

Even if you're not completely ready to let go, say it and pray it anyway. Say it and mean it as much as you can. You may not be speaking your reality at this point, but you are speaking your intention.

4. Ask God to change your heart. You have been real with God about your hurt and your anger. Now ask God to take them from you. You have renounced your claim to justice and satisfaction. All you want now is a heart free from the bonds of bitterness. Ask God to fill your heart with his forgiveness so you can forgive the one who harmed you.

5. Verbalize it. Say the words out loud to yourself. "Jim, I forgive you for cheating me." "Meghan, I forgive you for lying about me." "Pat, I give up my claim on you. You owe me nothing." "Ashley, I wish you well. I hope you find peace and goodness in this life."

Whatever it is, say it out loud and you will be amazed at the power of your words. We often wait for our feelings to change before we change our behavior. But there is power in changing our behavior and our words; our feelings often follow. That leads to the last step.

6. Extend a kindness to the person who hurt you. Recall the words of Ephesians 4:32: Be kind to one another. This may be the hardest of all. You may feel like a hypocrite. But do something kind for the person who hurt you, and you will begin to feel freedom.

You may tell the person that you have forgiven him or her. You may do that in person or in a letter. You may say something kind about him or her in the presence of others. You may send a gift whether you let him or her know it's from you.

If the person who hurt you is a spouse or a child or a friend, if possible open your heart to him or her. Let them in. In time, your heart will begin to change. A prisoner will be set free, and the prisoner will be you. Or in the words of Lydia Tillman, choose love and peace and when you do, you win.

Here is a word of caution and a word of encouragement. Just because you forgive someone, you do not necessarily need to reestablish the same kind of relationship that you had with him or her previously.

If your child has a drug problem and has stolen from you, you may have removed him from your home or told him that he's not welcome any longer. I hope you will be able to forgive him. But that doesn't mean that you need to invite him back into your home, not until he has gotten clean. You can forgive him, love him, and show him great kindness, but it's not wise for him to live with you again until he's working a program and has earned your trust. As long as he is actively using drugs, he's likely to steal and lie to support his habit. God said we need to forgive, not be foolish or naive.

If your spouse cheated on you, for your own sake you will need to forgive. But that does not mean that he or she can now be trusted. You can forgive someone and at the same time determine that he or she is not a person of character who can be faithful to their promises. We are to get rid of bitterness, not our powers of discernment.

Not every act of forgiveness results in reconciliation. But every act of grace brings healing to our hearts and makes us more like Christ.

For a final word of encouragement, we turn to the example of Rubin "Hurricane" Carter. On June 17, 1966, two men entered the Lafayette Grill in Paterson, New Jersey, and shot three people to death. Carter was a celebrated boxer, twenty-nine years old at the time. He and an acquaintance of his were falsely charged and wrongly convicted of the murders in a highly publicized and racially charged trial.

Carter maintained his innocence for nineteen years, until his convictions were set aside by a federal judge who declared that his prosecution had been "predicated upon an appeal to racism rather than reason, and concealment rather than disclosure."[7] As a free man, Carter reflected on how he chose to respond to the injustice he had suffered. After noting that the most productive years of his life had been stolen from him and that he had been deprived of seeing his children grow up, he stated that he had a right be bitter, but he chose not to be. In Carter's own words, he said:

> If I have learned nothing else in my life, I've learned that bitterness only consumes the vessel that contains it. And for me to permit bitterness to control or infect my life in any way whatsoever, would be to allow those who imprisoned me to take even more than the twenty-two years they've already taken.[8]

Your life is too important to be destroyed by the cruelty of others or the injustice you have experienced. Bitterness does nothing but "consume the vessel that contains it."

There is healing for you. There is a new life waiting for you. You can decide today to begin the process of forgiveness and be set free of your pain and anger to experience the joy of your salvation.

3

NEGATIVITY

Jesus left there and went to his hometown, accompanied by his disciples. When the Sabbath came, he began to teach in the synagogue, and many who heard him were amazed.

"Where did this man get these things?" they asked. "What's this wisdom that has been given him? What are these remarkable miracles he is performing? Isn't this the carpenter? Isn't this Mary's son and the brother of James, Joseph, Judas and Simon? Aren't his sisters here with us?" And they took offense at him.

Jesus said to them, "A prophet is not without honor except in his own town, among his relatives and in his own home." He could not do any miracles there, except lay his hands on a few sick people and heal them. He was amazed at their lack of faith.

(Mark 6:1-6)

It begins in the mind. What does? Just about everything. Success and failure. Happiness and misery. Hope and despair. They all begin in the mind. That's why you can put two people in the same situation, and they will react in completely different ways.

One of the gifts you receive as a pastor is being invited into the lives of people. After a while, you've seen just about everything. You've seen these things more than once, in fact, many times. It's a wonderful opportunity to learn about human nature—how we are all alike and how we're different.

In many ways, human beings are very similar. We all want to be somebody. We don't all want to be the CEO of a company or a movie star or even somebody who's up front and well known. But we all want to matter to someone. We all need to love and to be loved. And we all need to find something to do with our lives that gives us a sense of meaning and purpose.

But when it comes to living with joy, we are very different. I have known people who were dying of cancer, some long before they expected to leave this world, who were at the same time filled with joy. I think of Jim who worked in the oil field and coached his sons' Little League teams when they were young. He had stopped working just a few years before he was diagnosed. His disease was going to cut his life short and keep him from fulfilling many of the dreams he had for retirement.

I sat beside his bed less than two weeks before his death. Without any prompting from me, he began to tell me about his faith. He said, "When I heard the news, I wasn't mad or angry. Really, I smiled. I've had such a wonderful life, if the Lord was standing right here, there's nothing I could ask him for." He told me how he loved walking in the woods and how God often spoke to him there. His eyes filled with tears when he talked about how he loved Christmas more than any other time of the year "because at Christmas it seems the whole world is focused on Jesus." Then he said, "When I think back on the greatest joys in life, they all come back to Jesus."

Jim is one of many people I have known over the years who were full of joy when they could have been depressed and bitter. Others had lost their jobs or been mistreated by a spouse or had found themselves spending great amounts of time, energy, and money caring for a loved one who was disabled or ill. Yet they were in love with life and encouraged me and others by their example.

I have also known people who have everything, and they are miserable and find some reason to complain constantly. It seems they look for the worst in every situation. They find it if they can and imagine it if they can't. I sometimes have thought that it must make them happy to be so miserable. Except they're not happy.

In many ways, human beings are surprisingly similar. But it's amazing how different people are when it comes to living with joy. Two people can be in the same negative situation, and one focuses on her blessings and the other is fixated on his problems. Two other people can have the same blessings in their lives, and one is thankful while the other is worried that the good times won't last.

Even good Christian folks who believe the same things—what God is like, who Jesus is, how we become right with God, and how God wants us to live—two people can believe the same things and still have very different reactions to the same events. Why? Because it's not just what you think that matters. It's *how* you think.

This is a broad generalization, but it's true as far as it goes. Some of us tend to think in positive terms. Others of us have a natural inclination to see the proverbial glass as half empty. Life has taught me—my own life and the lives of hundreds of people I have counseled—that positive is better than negative.

Being positive doesn't mean ignoring reality. It doesn't mean pretending that everyone's really good on the inside, or that everything is beautiful if you just look at it the right way. You can be a realist and still be positive. Being positive simply means that we look for the good in every situation, believe that even our worst days come bearing gifts, and trust that God can bring a blessing out of every negative and hurtful situation we face. (After all, that is the great story we celebrate—God bringing the greatest good out of the worst evil.)

The bottom line is that joy is not determined by what has or has not happened in our lives, whether life has been fair or whether we have problems. Happy people have problems. Unhappy people have problems. All God's children have problems. The difference is that happy people refuse to let negativity fill their minds or rule over their spirits.

Let's look at the joy stealer of negativity. Where does it comes from, what does it do to us, and how can we overcome it?

Sources of Negativity

Where does a negative approach to life originate? Sometimes negativity comes from the people in our lives. This is especially true if we were surrounded by negative people when we were children. Our parents or the people who raised us have a huge impact on how we see the world. Children learn how to handle problems and how to think about life from their parents' words and by their example.

Dr. Frank Minirth and Paul Meier wrote, "Individuals who spend their entire childhood identifying with negativistic, chronically depressed parents are going to learn similar attitudes."[1] Our parents are "god figures" as we grow up. They are bigger, stronger, and wiser. We depend on them for our very existence. So we naturally look to them to learn about life. They teach us, with their words and by their example, what to expect out of life, how to react, what emotions are and are not acceptable to feel or to express. They even teach us how to feel about ourselves—whether we believe we possess worth and are deserving of love, or not. In many ways, the adults who raised us defined reality for us. If someone grows up with a negative, pessimistic parent, it will often affect that person and his or her ability to be positive and hopeful about life.

Later in life, the company we keep can have a similar effect. If you are surrounded by negative people who like to complain, it will rub off on you. Paul wrote to the Corinthians "Do not be misled: 'Bad company corrupts good character'" (1 Corinthians 15:33). The people with whom you associate will influence you, Paul says. If the people around you are negative, always looking for a reason to complain, you will find it a real battle to remain positive.

Another source of negativity are the events in life that wound us. We don't have to give in to their power, but hurtful, negative events often lead to a pessimistic attitude and a sense of hopelessness. Get burned in a relationship, get cheated in business, have your hopes and dreams come crashing down around you, and it becomes harder to be positive about the future.

Mark Twain wrote in *Following the Equator*, "We should be careful to get out of an experience only the wisdom that is in it—and stop there; lest we be like the cat that sits down on a hot stove-lid. She will never sit down on a hot stove-lid again—and that is well; but also she will never sit down on a cold one any more."[2]

Sometimes we learn too much from our negative experiences. They should teach us to think through our actions, take proper precautions, and prepare for the worst. But when we learn from negative events that we shouldn't dream, shouldn't take risks, shouldn't believe that the future can be better than the present, then we have learned too much, and we have become negative in the process.

One other source for a negative approach to life can be growing up in a dysfunctional family. Imagine a household in which one parent drinks and is never there for you. The other parent is difficult to predict—kind and loving one minute, critical and raging the next. Perhaps you don't have to imagine, because you've lived this reality. In such an environment, your needs are ignored. Perhaps you're told verbally and directly or indirectly by your family's actions that you aren't worthy of love and care. Growing up in such a home might very well lead you to become negative about yourself and about life. You will come to the conclusion that there is something wrong with you—you're not smart enough, good enough, or pretty enough to be to be happy. You live always thinking that you have to do more and be more than you are before you are deserving of joy.

Children in dysfunctional homes may also grow up with a need to protect themselves from future hurt and disappointment. They come to the conclusion, consciously or not, that they will never set themselves up to be disappointed or hurt again. It's easier and it feels safer to be negative and protect themselves from being let down again than it is to be positive, to hope that things might change, and to make themselves vulnerable again.

Whatever the cause, think negatively long enough and over time that will not just be the way you think. That's who you will become. You will live without joy. You may have a few moments of happiness, but not deep, enduring joy.

Let's look in detail at what negativity does to us and how we can overcome this joy stealer.

1. Negativity turns our opportunities into obstacles.

What's the difference between an obstacle and an opportunity? Our attitude—how we choose to see our situation.

My wife, Peggy, and I have some friends in Houston who own a very successful oil and gas company that employs scores of people. They are one of our favorite couples. Both of them are Christ-centered and generous with servant hearts.

The husband was a young man working for a major oil company in the 1980s when there was a huge downturn and people were losing their jobs. In these circumstances he could have thought, "I'm young and newly hired; I'm going to get laid off," and he probably would have been right. Instead, he went to his wife and said, "We've always talked about owning our own company. This seems like the perfect time to me. There are going to be a lot of properties on the market going cheap. If we can buy them now and make them more productive, when things turn around, we'll be off and running." And that's exactly what happened.

Today, they have made a great life for themselves and for others, and they have been able to support God's work around the world with their finances in transformative ways. Why? Because instead of seeing an obstacle, they saw an opportunity.

What determines how you see the situations you face? You do. What and how you think will shape whether you see obstacles or opportunities before you.

Will you see conflict with another person as an obstacle to your being happy, or as an opportunity to create a better relationship? Will you think of your disappointments as a reason to become bitter, or as an opportunity to learn and grow? Will you see the loss of a job as a crisis, or as an opportunity to rethink what you love to do and to reinvent yourself?

No one can answer those questions but you. But if you think negatively—choosing to see what's wrong in every situation or what could go wrong—you will miss out on many of the opportunities God brings your way, and you will create obstacles for yourself that don't even exist.

2. Negativity limits our potential.

Who's right? The person who says I can or the person who says I can't? It's a trick question. They both are.

Believe you can't be successful, can't overcome your problems, can't make a difference . . . and you won't be successful, overcome your problems, or make a difference.

The most successful people in the world, personally and professionally, are not necessarily the smartest, the best educated, the most gifted, or those who have been given every advantage. Usually they are fairly ordinary people with the extraordinary belief that they can learn what they need to learn, do what they need to do, work as hard as they need to work, and succeed if they just keep trying.

My wife is much more positive than I am. I'm a perfectionist by nature. Perfectionists see all the problems, all the things that might go wrong, all the reasons not to take a bold step and do something amazing.

Peggy is very different. A creative, challenging idea occurs to her and off she goes to make it happen. I tell her, "You don't know what you can't do, so you just go out and do it."

For years Peggy said, "Rob, you should write a book." And for years I'd respond, "That's crazy. Who'd read a book that I wrote? And even harder, who'd publish a book that I wrote?"

As it turns out, twenty years after she started bugging (I mean *encouraging)* me, this is the third book I've written. And one of the great joys of my life is hearing from people who have found comfort and strength in my previous books.

Who knows how God might use you if your first reaction to an idea wasn't *That's crazy, I could never do that.* What would happen if you didn't immediately dismiss your ideas for making the world better? What might come to pass if, instead of discounting your gifts, you claimed them and believed God could use them? What if, when people told you that you were really good at something— teaching, encouraging, art, hospitality, leadership—instead of thinking, *That's nuts,* you let yourself think for just a moment, *That might be God speaking to me*? What good could you do for the kingdom of God and for hurting people?

A great God created you in his own image with tremendous potential. You are intelligent enough, creative enough, and gifted enough to succeed at just about anything you set your mind to accomplish.

What most limits what you achieve with your life for others and for God? The limits you put on yourself. And nothing limits you as much as the negative thinking that says, "I could never do that."

You can know the immense joy of using your strengths for a purpose that is worthy of your life. You can know the joy that comes when you have given God and others the best you've got and you see the difference you have made.

Or you can decide before you even try that your obstacles are too big, the timing is all wrong, and your abilities are too small. Do that, and the spirit within you will be frustrated and unfulfilled, not because your gifts are inadequate but because your thinking is too negative.

3. Negativity hinders what God can do in our lives.

In Mark 6, Jesus returns to his hometown. This passage immediately follows Jesus' healing a woman who has been bleeding for twelve years and raising a young girl from the dead. But in Nazareth, "He could not do any miracles there, except lay his hands on a few sick people and heal them. He was amazed at their lack of faith" (Mark 6:5-6).

Jesus performed miracles everywhere he went, often healing great numbers of people. But he was unable to do as much in his hometown. Why? As Mark says, it was because of their lack of faith.

The people in Jesus' hometown refused to believe in him. At first they were impressed with his teaching, but then Mark says they took offense at him. "Jesus—he's the kid who used to live here, right? He's Mary's son. He was a carpenter when he left here, and now he claims that he can heal people and acts like he's a teacher with authority. No training, no credentials. Who does he think he is?"

Did Jesus have any less power in Nazareth than he had in other places? Did he possess any less compassion? Did he feel any less desire to heal the sick and relieve their suffering?

No. Only one thing was different in Nazareth. Rather than being filled with faith, the people were filled with negativity and skepticism.

The story is often recounted of Mother Teresa that, when she was a young nun, she told her superiors that she had a dream of building an orphanage for God. When they asked her what resources she possessed, she told them she had three pennies. When they chided her that she could not build an orphanage with three pennies, she responded, "Oh, I know that. But with God and three pennies, I can do anything."

We were made to have God doing his work in us and through us. Negativity limits that work and robs us of the joy that comes only when God is moving powerfully in our lives.

4. Negativity repels positive people and attracts negative people.

Have you ever noticed how many of the proverbs we quote contradict each other? Which one is right: "Out of sight out of mind" or "Absence makes the heart grow fonder"? It probably depends on the situation. Which is better advice: "Look before you leap" or "He who hesitates is lost"? Which should guide your life: "Better safe than sorry" or "Nothing ventured, nothing gained"? Again, it probably depends on the situation.

Here's a truth that doesn't depend on the situation. Negative people do not attract positive people. People who are looking for the good in life, full of faith, who believe they can overcome the challenges they face do not want to have anything to do with people who are constantly negative. They will not voluntarily spend any more time than they must with grumbling, complaining people.

And with good reason. In an article titled "Listening to Complainers Is Bad for Your Brain," *Inc. Magazine* refers to a Stanford study on the effects of listening to someone drone on about how bad things are. The article reports that "exposure to 30 minutes or more of negativity . . . actually peels away neurons in the brain's hippocampus," which helps with insight and problem solving.[3] Positive people know instinctively that listening to people who constantly complain will damage their brains and lower their intelligence. So they don't do it.

Complain all the time and be pessimistic about everything, and positive people who can help you dream more, do more, achieve more and be more won't have anything to do with you. They are not going to let your negativity damage their brains and destroy their spirits. Instead you will only attract other negative people who'd rather gripe about what's wrong than work to make things right.

A member of a church I served years ago was a good-hearted soul but constantly negative. When we entered into a capital campaign for a building project, he made it his mission in life to tell me all the negative things people were saying about the campaign. "Rob, I think you'd like to know that lots of people think" and he'd finish the sentence with some reason "lots" of people had reservations about the campaign. (By the way, most pastors figure out pretty early in their ministry that "lots of people" means "me, my spouse, and one of our friends.") He'd always end his report with these words: "I don't know why people come to me with all of this."

Finally I told him what I heard a pastor say at a conference. "Brother, people who carry garbage around are always looking for a place to unload it. And when they find a dump that will receive it, that's where they drop it off." Then I said, "For some reason it seems people have come to believe that you are that dump. I wonder why?"

Think negative, talk negative, and be only too happy to listen to what other negative people have to say, and you will draw grumbling, complaining people to you like flies. What you will not attract are eagles who can help you soar.

Decide which you want in your life—flies or eagles—and adjust your attitude accordingly.

5. Negativity will ruin your witness for Jesus.

When our boys were in elementary school, Peggy had a conference with one of their teachers. They met in a little room next to the principal's office. The principal saw them and joined them until the conversation was over. The teacher was the first one to step out into the hallway when the meeting ended. She immediately turned around, stepped back into the office with the principal and Peggy, and shut the door behind her. She was shaking.

She told the principal, "It's that woman. I'm not going out there until she leaves. I can't take it anymore."

The principal didn't have to ask who she was talking about. "Oh, don't let her get to you," she said. "Just say hi and keep walking." The teacher looked at my wife and said, "She's so negative. She's finds something wrong with everything, and she has to tell me all about it. I'm not even her child's teacher. I'm not going out there until she's gone."

My wife left first, with the teacher still in the office refusing to leave. As Peggy left, she looked down the hall only to discover that she knew the woman. She was a member of the church I was pastoring!

Do you know why unchurched people start going to church? Usually it's because they want to make some kind of positive change in their lives. They want to make a relationship better, discover how to live with peace and contentment, or overcome a bad habit that's a destructive force in their lives. They are looking for hope and for a reason to believe that tomorrow can be better than yesterday. One way or another, they're hoping to make a positive change in their lives.

What chance do you think the negative parent I just described had of bringing people to church who wanted to make their lives better? Little, if any. They may very well think that woman's church creates people like her. Even worse, they may conclude that Jesus creates people like her.

As Christians, some of our greatest joys in life come from helping others, especially helping them experience God's grace. Such joy may even come from leading them into a personal, saving relationship with Jesus. But if you complain constantly about how horrible your life is, or how awful "those idiots in Washington are," or how terrible your boss or your job is, then you will destroy your opportunity to help people who want to change their lives for the better. And you will rob yourself of one of the greatest joys you are meant to know.

How Can We Become More Positive?

If you want to become a more positive person, what can you do? There are some simple steps you can take. But just because they're simple doesn't mean they're easy. If you have gotten into the habit of being negative or catch yourself becoming that way, training yourself to be more positive will take some real work. You will need to monitor how you're doing, catch yourself when you fall back into old habits, and recommit to a more positive approach to life. But you can become more positive, and even a little change in your attitude will make a big difference in how you live.

1. ACCEPT RESPONSIBILITY FOR YOUR ATTITUDE.

Nobody can make you happy but you. And nobody can choose your attitude but you—not your spouse, your parents, your friends, or your pastor. You are responsible for your attitude. The good news is that if you are responsible for your attitude, you are also "response-able" to change your attitude.

The following statement has been attributed to many sources: "What lies behind us and what lies before us are tiny matters compared to what lies within us." What lies behind us—those are our past hurts and disappointments. What lies before us—those are the future challenges we will face. Whoever the original author was, he or she picked up on an important biblical truth. The power within us is more than sufficient to overcome whatever has or will come against us.

Here's another way of stating the same truth: It's not what happens to you, but what happens inside you that makes the difference. Much depends on your attitude, your faith, and your dependence on the One who lives in you who is "greater than the one who is in the world" (1 John 4:4). These will give you the power to overcome whatever comes against you.

You are a human being, not an automaton that can be programmed against your will by other people or the things that happen to you. You are not a microwave oven. People cannot come by and press your buttons and all of a sudden you have to heat up and go off. You can always choose how you respond, how you see the world, and whether you live with a negative, complaining spirit or with a heart that's positive and full of faith.

Am I saying you can change your actions and your life simply by accepting responsibility for your attitude and changing how you think? Absolutely. Think differently, and you will begin to act differently. Act differently, and you will begin to feel differently.

We sometimes think, *When my feelings change, then I'll be able to change how I act.* But that's not always true. Often, if you change how you act, your feelings will follow. Do something good, and you will begin to feel good. Do something positive, and the way you think will become more positive. We usually act on the theory that our behavior follows our feelings. You can live that way if you want to—at the mercy of your moods. Or you can discover the truth that your feelings will follow your actions if you take positive steps to make your life better.

There is immense power in the simple belief that you are responsible for your attitude. Believe that and act on that, and you will become a more positive person.

2. LOOK FOR THE GOOD AROUND YOU.

Negative people focus on what's going wrong. Positive people look for what's going right. Negative people concentrate on what they don't have. Positive people are grateful for what they do have.

Paul wrote: "Praise be to the God and Father of our Lord Jesus Christ, who has blessed us in the heavenly realms with every spiritual blessing in Christ" (Ephesians 1:3).

When Paul writes about our blessing in this passage, he doesn't refer to something that will happen in the future or even to something that is occurring in the present. He is describing a reality that has already taken place. "God . . . has blessed us." And with what? "With every spiritual blessing in Christ." Peace, joy, love, hope, strength, faith, forgiveness—God has already provided us with all of those gifts.

If we aren't experiencing these blessings, it's not because God hasn't given them to us. It's because there's a problem on our end. There's some attitude, some action, some error in our thinking that is preventing us from receiving what God has already given.

Of course, we're not always happy. Life is hard, and sometimes it's more than that—it's painful and unfair. It's OK to get down. But if we are not generally experiencing and walking in the blessings that God has already given us, then we have to ask, "Why?"

Several years ago, I watched Bob Costas interview the comedian Milton Berle on the show *Later*. Berle said that after he had retired from show business, he still wanted to put a smile on people's faces, and he would often entertain at homes for senior citizens. He would begin with a show in the commons area. Afterward, he would take some time and walk into the rooms of people who had been unable to get out of bed and join the others.

He said he once entered a room and saw a dear woman in bed who could hardly lift her head off the pillow. He knelt next to her bed and said, "M'am, do you know who I am?" The woman stared at him but didn't say anything. He flashed his big smile at her and asked again, "Dear, do you know who I am?" The woman responded, "No. But if you ask the lady at the front desk, she can tell you."

In case you have forgotten who you are, let me tell you. You are a child of God. You have been given every spiritual blessing in Christ. That means you are blessed enough to grateful. You are bright enough to be successful. You possess more than enough to be happy. And you are loved enough by your Father to be confident and secure. That's who you are.

The apostle Paul, who suffered more and endured greater hardships for preaching the gospel than we will ever face, gives us this promise: "We know that in all things God works for the good of those who love him, who have been called according to his purpose" (Romans 8:28). Not everything that happens is good. This verse doesn't say that. There is evil and injustice and suffering in the world, and you will experience your share before your life is over.

But here's God's promise to you. He's in the midst of what you're going through. He's working for your good. Look for what God is doing. You may catch a glimpse of how God is working on your behalf. If not, claim this promise and keep looking. Don't give in to pessimism and cynicism and fear, because one day you will see what God was doing to bring good out of bad. God will have the last word over every situation in your life, and that word will be good. Look for it and you'll find it—if not now, then later. And instead of becoming negative and bitter, you'll live with a thankful heart and a positive mind.

3. INVENTORY YOUR INFLUENCERS.

What's influencing you and your attitude? If you're like most folks, more than anything else it's the television shows and movies you watch; the books, magazines, and websites you read; the music you listen to; and the people you spend time with.

You can watch, read, and listen to anything you desire. You can hang out with anyone you wish. But we need to be aware that they are influencing how we see the world and ourselves. The question we need to ask is, "Are they helping me become the more positive, Christ-centered, person of faith I desire to be?"

Paul addressed a question like this in his first letter to the Corinthians. Some in the Corinthian church had misunderstood the message of grace; they believed they could continue to live the way they had before coming to faith in Christ. In the first eleven verses of 1 Corinthians 6, Paul reminds them that they have been cleansed of their old ways and given a new identity and a new nature in Christ. Consequently, they could not live the same old way. He then quotes what appears to be a slogan of theirs followed by some godly wisdom. "'I have the right to do anything,' you say—but not everything is beneficial" (1 Corinthians 6:12).

Even if something is permissible, that doesn't mean it's beneficial. Something may be morally acceptable in the sight of God, but it might not be helpful to our walk with Christ. So along with asking the question, "Is opening my life to the influence of this thing or person acceptable in God's sight?," we also need to ask, "Will this help me be the person I want to be?"

I'm not telling you what to read or watch or whom to associate with. But it's wise to take inventory of what you're inviting into your heart and mind. Look at what you're looking at. Spend some time thinking about the people you spend time with. Earlier in this chapter I quoted Paul where he told the Corinthians, "Bad company corrupts good character" (1 Corinthians 15:33). The company we keep will influence us—the way we live and the attitude we possess. A study conducted at the University of Warwick, released in the fall of 2017, discovered that "both good and bad moods can be 'picked up' from friends. . . . Evidence suggests mood may spread from person to person via a process known as social contagion."[4]

For years I had a running partner who made certain I hit the trails every day whether I felt like running or not. I once noticed that though we were different heights and our legs were different lengths, our strides were exactly the same. For six miles, we matched each other step for step. It didn't happen because we thought about it or planned it that way. It wasn't because that stride was natural for either of us. It happened simply because when you're running with someone, it's normal and it's easier to get in sync, to get in step with each other.

It works the same way in life. You tend to get in step with those you're making your journey with. You may not have intended to do so. You may not even realize that you've done it. But whether it's their moods, their attitudes, or their values, you will be influenced by those you spend the most time with.

You may want to spend time with negative people who need to be encouraged. You may want to help them and lift them up. As followers of Jesus, we should do such things with love. But be careful that you don't become negative yourself.

Imagine yourself standing on a table and the person you want to help is on the floor. You reach down to pull him up. He takes your hand and tries to pull you down. Who's likely to win?

Some influencers in your life will cause you to dream big and live large. Spend as much time as possible with them. Others will cause you to dream small and become cynical. Be careful around them. It's always easy to go low with our attitude and our goals. It's harder to aim high. Be intentional about who you give access to your spirit.

4. TAKE CONTROL OF YOUR TONGUE.

"The tongue has the power of life and death, and those who love it will eat its fruit" (Proverbs 18:21). The words you speak will feed your spirit. You will eat their fruit—either for good or for bad.

Do this, will you? Smile. And hold it for ten seconds. Smile, take a deep breath and hold it.

Feel better? I bet you do. It's hard to smile and feel bad. It's hard to frown and feel good. It's also hard to speak positively and feel negatively. And it's hard to speak negatively and at the same time feel good.

I hope you will get up every morning and say, "It's going to be a great day." Maybe you've heard the difference between an optimist and a pessimist is that when an optimist wakes up, she says, "Good morning, God." The pessimist says, "Good God. Morning."

I hope you'll get up every morning and say, "Good morning, God. It's going to be a great day. I am blessed. I am loved. You are working for my good. Today, something great is going to happen, and I'm going to look for it."

You may think, "But isn't it a lie to say that if I don't feel that way?" I'll tell you what a lie is. A lie is for you to know that God is in your life; to know that Jesus has died for you and you have been forgiven and given a second chance; to know that the power of the Holy Spirit is living in you; to know that when you leave this world, you're going to spend eternity with God—and then someone looks at you the wrong way, somebody says something you don't like, or something doesn't go your way, and you begin to spend your energy on negative thoughts and let yourself feel miserable. A lie is to have known God's goodness and nevertheless to complain that life is unfair, you'll never be happy, and things will never change. That's the lie you should worry about believing and telling yourself.

God is at work in your life, and God's presence, your salvation, the power of the Holy Spirit, and your eternity with God are all true regardless of how you feel about them. They are never a lie to speak or to believe.

The Book of Lamentations was written in one of the darkest moments in the history of Israel. Jerusalem had been laid waste. The temple had been destroyed. Death and starvation filled the city. The author, usually thought to Jeremiah, confesses his desperation. But with his next breath he states, "The steadfast love of the LORD never ceases; his mercies never come to an end; they are new every morning" (Lamentations 3:22-23 ESV).

The prophet knows what he sees. He knows what he feels. But there is something he trusts even more than what his eyes or his emotions tell him. He trusts the goodness of God. Even when he doesn't feel it, he speaks it. "The steadfast love of the LORD never ceases."

When does the psalmist say, "The LORD is my shepherd, I shall not want" (Psalm 23:1, RSV)? It's when he is walking through "the valley of the shadow of death" (23:4 RSV). When does Paul proclaim, "I can do all things through him who strengthens me" (Philippians 4:13 NRSV)? It's not after a great victory when he feels compelled to celebrate, but when he is writing to the Philippians from a prison cell.

It's possible to believe the truth and to declare the truth even when your circumstances and your feelings tell you something different. If you want to take control of your attitude, take control of your words. Learn the promises of God. Memorize them. Speak them. And see if it's not true that the words you speak will feed your soul.

You can let negative people, negative events, and a negative world form your spirit. If you do, you will live without the joy that is yours in Christ.

Or you can accept responsibility for your attitude, look for what is good, bring the right kind of influencers into your life, and let the powerful, positive truths of God's word determine how you think, what you say, and how you live. Do that, and even in the midst of difficult times, you will be able to live with faith and joy.

4

BUSYNESS

*Our days may come to seventy years,
    or eighty, if our strength endures; . . .
    for they quickly pass, and we fly away. . . .
Teach us to number our days,
    that we may gain a heart of wisdom.*
                                    (Psalm 90:10, 12)

You are limited. Why would I begin a chapter in a book about joy with that statement? Because accepting your limitations is foundational to living a meaningful, exciting, and joyful life.

I know it doesn't come across as a catchy or inspiring slogan. "Accept your limitations." Coaches don't go into the locker room, down by fourteen points, and fire their players up with the phrase, "I want you to go out there this second half and accept your limitations!" You won't find "You Are Limited" on motivational posters. It won't sell any T-shirts. You'll never see it on a bumper sticker.

What sells is "No limits." "If you can dream it, you can do it." "The only limits are in your mind." Those are the messages that fire people up, and I know why. Those statements speak to the desire within us to do and to be more.

I believe you can do just about anything you decide to do. A great God made you in his image. You are intelligent and creative. You have an incredible ability to learn and grow and persevere until you succeed at just about any goal you set for yourself.

I believe you can do just about anything. But I don't believe you can do everything. If you try—if you don't concentrate your efforts on a limited number of important goals—you will never know the satisfaction that comes only when you have purposefully and passionately invested your efforts into the causes that you believe matter most. Instead, you will live a scattered, unfocused life that is rarely productive and almost never creates the deep joy that comes from knowing God has used us powerfully to spread his kingdom.

You can do more than you think you can. But you can't do everything. Why? Because you are limited. Everyone is. The hours in our day are limited. The energy in our bodies is limited. The talents we possess are limited.

So is the time we have on this earth. The psalmist wrote, "Our days may come to seventy years, or eighty, if our strength endures; . . . for they quickly pass, and we fly away" (Psalm 90:10).

Some of us are given more time than others. A friend of mine told me about attending a woman's 104th birthday. He said to her, "Miss Mae, 104 years, that's an awfully long time." She said to him, "Jimmy, from where you are, looking forward, it sure is. But from where I am, looking back, it's amazing how quickly it has all gone by."

No matter how many years we're given, they will one day come to an end. When they do, we are very likely to look back on them and be surprised at how quickly they went by.

How does the psalmist respond when he acknowledges the limited time he has on earth? He prays. "Teach us to number our days, that we may gain a heart of wisdom" (Psalm 90:12).

We don't have forever to figure out what's most important. We don't have forever to do something with our lives that matters. We don't have forever to make things right or to get our lives in order. Our time on this planet is limited. So, the psalmist says, we'd better be wise with the choices we make.

One response to the brevity of our lives and the other limitations we face is to attempt to do all we can as quickly as we can for as long as we can. Every good thing we can think to do, we do it. Every opportunity for fun and happiness, off we go. Burn our candle at both ends. Even if it does not last the night, we will stay busy and, hopefully, happy.

But is that the way of wisdom? Or is there a better way to live a full and exciting life and experience deep and lasting joy?

Talk with people who are always busy. They are always running from one activity to another, always doing whatever they are asked to do. They are always looking for and rushing to that next high that promises to make them happy. Usually what you find are people who are frazzled and frustrated. Often they are uncertain what they have accomplished at the end of the day. Exhausted and weary, they wonder why they are unhappy and unfulfilled. They are allowing busyness to steal their joy.

You are limited. That's a given. You want your life to count. That's true of most people, and I assume it's true for you as well. So, how do people who are limited and who want their lives to matter live wisely and experience joy?

1. We must understand that priorities are essential.

James Allen wrote a well-known statement that is often quoted: "You are today where your thoughts have brought you; you will be tomorrow where your thoughts take you."[1] It's a compelling statement. It reminds us how powerful the mind is, and it encourages us to think carefully about our lives. It's a good line. It's just not exactly true.

Your thoughts don't take you anywhere, not really. Your thoughts show you where you can go, but they don't take you there. Everyone who has taken a shower has had a brilliant thought.[2] Everyone who has taken a nap has dreamed a dream. Everyone who has taken a walk has envisioned a better life. Thinking, dreaming and envisioning are important. They show you where you can go, but they don't take you there.

A better line than Allen's is: You are today where your decisions have brought you; you will be tomorrow where your decisions take you.

The decisions you make—make you. The decisions you act on; the decisions you live by; the decisions you make about what's most important—those decisions are what move you forward and determine the life you live.

Decisions are our priorities taking on flesh. Every decision says we have found something worthy of our time, energies, finances, and lives. Whenever we make a decision, we demonstrate that something comes prior to the other opportunities we may have. Our decisions are the most concrete form of our priorities.

Priorities are an admission that we are limited. Our time, our energy, our finances, and our talents are all limited. We may wish we could do everything. But once we accept our limitations, we give up the illusion that we can have and do it all. We realize we must choose wisely what we do with the time and the talents we possess. We recognize that priorities are essential if we want to live wisely and do something with our lives that matters.

Priorities help us because they allow us to say "no" to "the good things" that often get in the way of our doing "the best things." Many people are cursed with competence. They can do many things well. You may be one of those people. If you take on a task, you complete it. You give it your best. You are committed to excellence. You know how to get things done, and you don't let people down. If you say you'll do something, you do it and you do it well.

Once people discover this about you, they will come a' knockin'. They will ask you to help them with charity events, community projects, and ministries at church. Because you are a good person and you want to help people, and because you are a Christian and believe you are here to make a difference, you will be inclined to say "yes." Good for you. And bad for you. It's bad for you because you cannot say "yes" to every good request and still complete the few best things that God has called you to do. You simply can't say yes to everything, and you shouldn't try.

How do you make certain that you do what's most important instead of the many good things that people may want you to do? You must do what is very difficult for many people. You must learn to say "no."

Years ago I read this line, and I have always loved it. "The truly free man is the one who will turn down an invitation to dinner without giving an excuse."[3]

I bet you can't do it. "Rob, would you and Peggy like to come over this Friday for dinner?" "No." "Do you have another invitation?" "No." "You tired and just need some time to yourself?" "Not really." "Going to be out of town?" "No."

Try it the next time you're invited out and you don't want to go. Just say "no." I bet you can't do it. You will lie, if you're like most people. You will break one of the Ten Commandments rather than be honest and just say "no."

You might come up with some excuse that may not be an outright lie, but it's not really the truth. "Uh, my spouse may have something planned for this Friday. I'll get back to you." "My daughter might be coming home from college this weekend." (It could happen.) "Don't know if you've heard, but there's been some talk about a Zombie apocalypse planned for this Friday, and we're going to hunker down and not take any chances. Probably won't happen. But, you know, just in case, we're going to stay close to home."

It's hard to say "no," especially when it's actually a good cause that you're asked to support. Why would you ever refuse to help with something that's worthwhile? Because you are limited, and you cannot do everything. If you try, you're going to be stressed out and frustrated. When you go to meet God, your deepest regret will not be that you didn't do a lot of good things. But it may very well be that you didn't do those few things that God put you on earth to achieve with your life.

Priorities empower us to say "no," not because we don't want to help, but because we know that we are limited. Priorities allow us to accept the reality that if we give our time and our energy to every good cause, we will very likely fail to complete those few essential tasks we are meant to accomplish with our lives. Priorities give us permission to say "no" when we should.

I have determined what is most important for me to accomplish with my life, including a growing relationship with God, being the kind of husband and father my wife and sons deserve, serving the congregation I love faithfully, helping to renew my denomination, and staying healthy. Truthfully, if I do all of that well, I don't have time for much else. As long as I remember those are my priorities, I can say "no" to what for me are "lesser things."

I have learned the power of simply saying, "I wish I could, but I can't." Maybe I could actually do what I'm being asked to do. It's not impossible for me to wedge it into my schedule. But if I can't do it and still complete what I believe are God's priorities for my life, then I can't do it. I don't make excuses or give explanations for not being able to do what someone wants me to do. If it gets in the way of what I have decided is most important (including being mentally and physically healthy), I tell them, "I wish I could, but I can't." And I don't. People never ask for an explanation, and I cannot tell you how freeing it is to be able to say "no" and leave it at that. It's not because I don't want to help others. It's because I don't want to fail in accomplishing what God has put me here to do. Priorities empower us to say "no" to some things, perhaps many things, so we can say "yes" to what's most important.

You may not feel comfortable telling people you can't do what they're asking you to do when it's physically possible for you to do so. If that's the case, perhaps you have not really come to grips with the reality that you are limited. Or you may believe that you are here on earth to be a nice person, help out where you can, or have people like you. But that would be selling yourself far too short. You are here to make a contribution that only you can make. You are here to fulfill a mission and to maximize your gifts and your time for God's kingdom. Please understand that you cannot do that if you say "yes" every time you are asked to help someone. You cannot do that if you pursue every idea that comes into your head or every opportunity that looks like fun. Decide you are here to discover your God-given purpose and to accomplish it. Once you do, you will realize the value of priorities and the necessity of saying "no," and you will discover the joy that comes from making the most of your life within your natural limitations.

Priorities also help us overcome our tendency to become distracted and coast. It is so easy to plateau in life. Spiritually, we lose our focus, and we begin to drift. Relationally, we quit working on our marriages or on our relationship with our children. Physically, we stop doing what it takes to stay in shape. Professionally, we rely on past successes and stop developing new skills.

Physical fitness and professional development are important. But I'm more concerned with our spiritual growth and our relationships with others. If you're like I am, it is so easy to become distracted from what matters most.

Distractions are all around us: the Internet, social media, 800 cable stations, news programs that spend as much time on trivia as they do on what's important and significant. We live in a world of distractions. Sometimes it's hard to determine what really matters; and even if we do, it's hard to stay focused on those things.

What's the best way to overcome the distractions that take away our focus and our passion? Determine what is truly important and keep those few goals before us like a beacon in the darkness, calling us forward. Know what your priorities are, remind yourself what they are, and recommit yourself to them daily.

You cannot do everything. But you can do what is essential for a useful and joyous life. You can control where you put your focus. You cannot control whether life is fair to you. You cannot control whether people like you. You cannot control the economy or the stock market. You cannot control drunk drivers or cancer. Eventually, as they grow older, you discover that you cannot control your children and the decisions they make. But you do have absolute control over what's most important in life—where you focus your thoughts, your energy, and your talents.

People without priorities just go with the flow. They coast through life. The problem is you never coast uphill. You never get to a higher place in your relationship with God, in your relationships with others, or in your professional life by coasting. The only way you can coast for any length of time is if you're going downhill.

People don't coast to greatness. They don't coast into an impactful life. They don't coast into doing God's work in the world. And they don't coast into joy.

Living without priorities is easy. It requires no work or effort. You don't have to think about what's important. You won't have make tough decisions about what to say "yes" or "no" to. You'll never need to sacrifice for a cause you believe in. Coasting through life is an easy way to go. But it's not the way of wisdom.

Wisdom tells me I have one chance to live well. I have one chance to be the husband my wife deserves. I have one opportunity to be the father my sons need. I have one life to make a difference, to fulfill God's will for my life, and to glorify the Savior who died for me. Wisdom tells me that I have one chance to tell a story with my life that I can be proud of. And wisdom tells me I will never live that life and I will never know real joy if I allow myself to become distracted by busyness and begin to coast.

2. Living with a heart of wisdom requires that we have the right priorities.

You can have priorities and live for your priorities. But if they are not priorities that create a life that matters, you've wasted your life. If you don't think about your priorities, if you're not intentional in developing your own definition of success, you're likely to adopt the same priorities that drive our culture and the people around you.

When a friend points to someone and says, "Do you know him? No? He's Bill Jones. He's very successful." What does your friend mean by "he's very successful"? Does your friend mean that Bill Jones is a great father?

Or that he's a loving and caring husband? Or that he has helped many others succeed in life? Does your friend mean Bill Jones worked to overcome his impatience and his anger and has grown into a more Christlike person?

No, your friend doesn't mean any of those things. In fact, he or she may not know anything about Bill Jones's personal life. All your friend knows is that the guy has made a lot of money, lives in a big house, and drives an expensive car. You know that's what your friend means when he or she says Bill Jones is very successful because you don't even think to ask, "Really? A success in what way?" Instead you ask, "Really? What does he do?"

There is a cultural assumption that is revealed in the way we talk and in the terms we use. We often imply through our speech and our attitudes that professional advancement and amassing wealth is what makes a person successful.

We even make statements like, "He's worth a lot." Think about what that statement implies. It suggests that a person with a lot of money is worth more than a laborer who comes home dead tired every evening but still helps his kids do their homework. Or he's worth more than the schoolteacher who is investing her life in children and will never make a third of his salary. Or he's worth more than the single mom who takes on two jobs so her children can go to college. Our words reflect a high priority that we place on financial wealth.

I want the members of my congregation to experience professional advancement and financial success. Even if they didn't pay my salary, I would want them to do well at work.

But here's my point. Our culture is always pushing us to work more, achieve more, and make more. Why? Because that's how you get more, and the more you get the more successful you are—and the more you're worth. If we do not think through our values, if we do not purposefully and carefully choose our priorities, we are likely to live by the same values our culture promotes, and we'll end up as driven and as unhappy as everyone else.

In the past, I have given a talk on spiritual growth to many groups that began with the question, "What do you want out of life?" I don't begin with that question anymore. I kept getting the same answer, and it was so discouraging. The answer I got consistently was, "I want to be happy." That was their answer. "I just want to have a happy life."

I wouldn't have minded so much if I had been speaking to nonbelievers. But these were Christians, and some had been Christians for many years. How did they ever decide that being happy should be the top priority of their lives?

Just so you'll know, I'm all for happiness. I like being happy. I like making other people happy. I want you to be happy.

But if you read the New Testament, there's no way you can miss the message that happiness isn't the main thing. Jesus did not die on the cross to make us happy. He died to make us holy. He told us to take up a cross and deny ourselves. The Scriptures tell us over and over to rejoice in our sufferings because our struggles and our pain give us the opportunity to grow in character and faith.

Aren't we meant to be joyful? Of course, we are. But joy in the Bible comes from our relationship with God and from the assurance he is with us. It's not a goal we pursue or a state of being that we achieve. Happiness is the result of following Christ, growing in character and serving a purpose greater than ourselves. Joy is the by-product of living well, not a prize we can snatch.

So, if that's what the Bible teaches, how did these followers of Christ I spoke to decide that what they wanted most out of life was to be happy? They got it from their culture.

Dartmouth Professor Darrin McMahon argues that happiness rather than service to God or a life of virtue has now come to be seen as the ultimate aim of life. He has said: "We no longer live our lives according to beauty or honor or virtue. We want to live in order to be happy."[4]

The search for happiness has become an obsession. Ruth Whippman, author of *America the Anxious*, writes: "Americans as a whole invest more time and money and emotional energy in the explicit pursuit of happiness than any other nation on earth." [5] Whippman writes that, according to independent market research, "the systematic packaging and selling of happiness in the form of books, DVDs, webinars, and courses [is an industry] estimated to be worth around ten billion dollars, roughly the same size as Hollywood, the other great purveyors of happy-ever-after."[6]

Our culture tells us we should expect to be happy. Our marriages should make us happy—and our jobs and our cars and our churches and our next cup of coffee from Starbucks.

This gets at the heart of why it bothers me so much when I ask Christian people what they want out of life and they say "to be happy." It's because they're getting their priorities from the world. They have turned to our hedonistic, materialistic culture to determine the purpose of their lives. Certainly they are unaware of what they have done, but instead of looking to the life of Jesus, the message of the Bible, or the character of God, folks who have been in the church for decades have allowed our self-obsessed, me-first culture to define their priorities.

You may have heard the term "cultural Christian." In case you're not familiar with it, it's not a compliment. There's no better definition of a cultural Christian than someone who believes in Jesus and at the same time just wants to be happy and believes they'll find happiness the same way the world does. We may love Jesus, read the Bible, go to church, and pray at meals. But if we want what the world wants, live like the world lives, and make decisions with the same priorities as the world does—to be happy—we have bought the world's lie that Jesus may save our souls, but it's the culture that tells us the purpose of life and how to achieve it.

It is foolish and it is dangerous to make being happy your life goal, just as it is to make the pursuit of wealth your life goal. It's dangerous because if your goal is happiness in the moment, you will not go through the difficult challenges of life and bear the suffering that is required to grow in character and faith. It is foolish because making happiness the purpose of your life does not produce a happy life.

Ruth Whippman reports that even though Americans spend more time and money than anyone else in the pursuit of happiness, surveys consistently find that we are some of the least happy people in the developed world. One study reported that we are less happy than the citizens of Rwanda. On top of that, according to the World Health Organization, we are by far the most anxious people on the planet, with nearly one-third of people in this country likely to suffer from an anxiety disorder in their lifetime.[7]

If we could catch happiness by chasing after it, or buy it with money, or attain it by reading books and attending conferences, we Americans would be the happiest people on earth. It would be Disney World all the time.

But it doesn't work that way. University College London professor of psychology Adrian Furnham put it this way: "(Happiness) is like soap in the bath. The more you try to grab it the more cloudy the water; the more difficult it is to find."[8] In fact, a series of studies conducted at UC Berkeley discovered that the more people value and seek after happiness, the more likely they are to be unhappy, anxious, and depressed.[9]

That's not surprising really. Jesus taught us that the fullness of life comes not from focusing on ourselves, but from forgetting ourselves and serving others.

Priorities alone do not produce a truly productive or joyful life. If you stay busy chasing after wealth or happiness, you will not experience joy. If you busy yourself with doing more, achieving more, getting more, you are likely to discover just how miserable a human being can become. Without the right priorities, busyness will steal the joy from your life.

So, how do we develop right priorities?

3. Right priorities come from a right understanding of who we are.

Who we are tells us a great deal about what we are to do with our lives. Look at how an object is designed, and you can come up with a pretty good idea of its purpose. Look at a hammer; its design tells you its purpose is not to saw boards. Study the design of a desk chair, and you can be pretty certain that its creator did not intend for people to sleep on it. Compare a dachshund and a Labrador retriever and you can fairly well surmise they were not bred for the same purpose.

What about human beings? What does our design tell us about our purpose and what should be our priorities?

First, we are created beings. Why begin there? Because that's where the Bible begins. "God said, 'Let us make humankind in our image . . .'" (Genesis 1:26 NRSV).

We human beings exist because God created us. Christians may debate just exactly how God brought us into being, but the Scriptures teach that we are not here by chance. A purposeful God intentionally created us. The psalmist states what is taught throughout the Bible: "Your hands made me and formed me" (Psalm 119:73).

You are a created being, brought into existence by God himself. That should tell you something about your purpose and your priorities.

In John's vision of heaven, he witnesses the twenty-four elders falling before the throne of God and crying out, "Thou art worthy, O Lord, to receive glory and honour and power: for thou hast created all things, and for thy pleasure they are and were created" (Revelation 4:11 KJV).

Everything God created, he created for his pleasure, and that includes you. You were created to bring joy to the heart of God.

You might think that existing for God's pleasure means that you are here to be his servant and do his will. And that's part of it. But if you have children, you know there's more to this verse than that. We don't bring children into existence so they will be our servants and do our will. And unless we're pretty sick, that's not how our children primarily bring joy to our hearts.

If you're a father, my guess is you didn't sit around with your wife and say, "You know, ten years from now it would bring me pleasure to have someone else mow the yard. Why don't we have a child?" If you're a mother, I bet you didn't think to yourself, "This housework is becoming a real drag. Having someone else do it for me would bring me pleasure," and then shout out, "Dear, either get me a maid or get me a baby because I want somebody else to start cleaning this house."

No, you had children because you had love in your heart you wanted to share. The very idea of raising a child and sharing life with him or her brought you pleasure. And after your child was born, nothing brought you more joy than holding your child, seeing his face, watching her take her first steps, and eventually hearing the words, "I love you." As your children grew older, nothing brought you as much pleasure as having conversations with them when they would open their hearts and share their lives with you and you were able to share your life with them. Nothing.

You were created for God's pleasure. And nothing gives him more pleasure than your responding to his invitation to become his child and grow in your relationship with him. God wants to share life with you the way a loving mother or father would share life with their children.

John's Gospel tells us: "The true light that gives light to everyone was coming into the world. He was in the world, and though the world was made through him, the world did not recognize him. He came to that which was his own, but his own did not receive him. Yet to all who did receive him, to those who believed in his name, he gave the right to become children of God" (John 1:9-12).

You were created to become a child of God and to have a personal relationship with him. Miss that, and no matter what else you may accomplish, you will have missed the greatest purpose and the greatest joy of life.

When you think about priorities, the place to begin is not so much with what you need to do, but who you need to be. You were created to be a child of God who knows the Father and who has a growing, personal relationship with him.

In John 1 and all throughout the Bible, the message is consistent. We do not become God's child by being good enough, or by going to church enough, or by trying to follow the Ten Commandments.

This passage says we become a child of God when we "receive him"—when we believe in his name.

What does it mean to believe in the name of Jesus? The name *Jesus* means "the Lord saves." Believing in his name means we believe we need a Savior. We believe that because of our sinfulness we can never do enough to make ourselves right with God. We owe a debt we cannot pay. But we believe that Jesus is the Savior who can do for us what we cannot do for ourselves. He can pay our debt, atone for our sins, and clothe us with his righteousness. We receive Jesus when we stop trusting ourselves and our efforts for salvation, and instead we trust solely in what Christ has done for us through his sinless life, his death, and his resurrection.

I often tell my church that "life is about relationships." I believe that because it's what Jesus taught—there's nothing more important than our relationships with other people except our relationship with God. Why? Because that's the reason we were created. God loves us, and he wants to be in a deep, personal relationship with us. That's the reason Jesus came into the world—so we could "become children of God." God has such deep affection for us that he desires us to be his children, able to experience the reality of his presence and his love in our lives. We enter that relationship when we put saving faith in Jesus. Each of us was created for this relationship, and nothing else can fill this deepest longing within our hearts.

The Bible also tells us that we are spiritual beings. There's more to being a spiritual being than we can delve into here. What I want to get across by saying we're spiritual beings at this point is simply this: You and I need a sense of purpose in our lives.

Back to Genesis 1: "God said, 'Let us make humankind in our image. . . .' So God created humankind in his image" (verses 26-27 NRSV).

We are made in God's image. We have a spiritual nature. And because we are spiritual beings, we crave meaning and purpose. We want to live for something that truly matters.

In Ecclesiastes 3:11 we are told: "He [God] has also set eternity in the human heart." That's why the pleasures of the flesh are never enough to fulfill the longings within us. That's why material possessions can't bring us lasting joy. That's why amassing power so often leaves people unhappy and cynical. That's why professional success causes even those at the top to cry out, "Is this all there is?"

Have you ever wondered why people who have everything can feel so empty inside? It's because we are spiritual beings. We yearn for something more than the prizes and the pleasures of this world can provide. We ache to live for something that matters and that will matter for eternity.

You are never bigger than the purpose you give your life to. If you give your life to material success, you'll never be bigger than money and stuff. If you dedicate your life to being respected and admired, you'll never be more than a little mound of pride. If you live for physical pleasure, you will never be more than an unsatisfied piece of flesh.

But if you want to be who you were created to be—if you want to know the immense pleasure of living the life you were destined for—you must live for an eternal purpose that honors God and does his work in the world. That purpose must be the priority of your life.

You are a spiritual person with eternity in your heart. Live for anything else, and you will be less than you were meant to be. You will never know the deep joy you were meant to experience from being used for a great purpose.

George Bernard Shaw was an Irish playwright who was the first person in history to be awarded both a Nobel Prize in literature and an Oscar. He was also a skeptic and a critic of religion. But his approach to life is so much closer to what the gospel teaches than the "I just want to be happy" mentality that we find in so many Christians in the West.

He wrote: "This is the true joy in life—being used for a purpose recognized by yourself as a mighty one; . . . being a force of Nature instead of a feverish selfish little clod of ailments and grievances complaining that the world will not devote itself to making you happy."[10] And in another place, "Life is no 'brief candle' for me. It is a sort of splendid torch which I have got hold of for the moment, and I want to make it burn as brightly as possible before handing it on to future generations."[11]

Look how the first passage begins: "This is the true joy in life." Joy. What brings joy? Living for a purpose that is "a mighty one." What is life? Shaw writes that it's a "splendid torch" that we have hold of for a brief moment. What robs our joy? Making life about ourselves and our momentary happiness or unhappiness instead of seeing life as a trust that we must steward for the good of others.

You are a spiritual being. Eternity is within your heart. Do not settle for a purpose that is small and worldly. No matter how great your success, how much you achieve, or how busy you stay, it will never be enough to fill that place in your heart that longs to live for a purpose that matters forever. Make that your priority.

I believe the purpose you were meant to live for is in your heart. Right now. God put it there when he created you. You can refer to it as your "calling." If you discover it and use it to focus your energy and your gifts like a magnifying glass does the rays of the sun, then even though you are limited, you will be able to accomplish something truly great for God and for others.

It's there inside your heart: something you care about deeply. There is some need, some cause, some issue, some group of people that your heart is especially tender toward. It's the answer to the question, "If I could accomplish any one thing for God, what would I do?" It's that need that causes you to cry out inside, "Somebody should do something about that." It's that issue that makes your voice rise and the words come quicker when you begin to talk about it. It has that effect on you because it's part of who you are. It's part of your heart, and it's part of your heart because God put it there when he created you.

Years ago, I went with several members of our church to India to discern how God might have us invest in caring for the poor there and in sharing the hope of the gospel with people who had never heard of Jesus.

The trip was amazing. India is overwhelming in every way, from the people to the traffic, the colors, the smells, the sights, and the poverty.

But it was something I read while I was there that literally stopped me in my tracks. It was a statement made by Mohandas Gandhi. What Gandhi accomplished with his life is difficult to fathom. He determined that he would free India from British rule. At the height of its power, the British Empire was the largest empire the world has ever seen. During Gandhi's lifetime, it held sway over a quarter of the world's population and nearly a fourth of the world's land mass.

British India was the empire's most valuable possession, "the Jewel in the Crown." India and its resources were integral to Britain's strength and a primary reason for the empire's continuing wealth.

Gandhi decided that he would cause the British to leave, just walk away from its greatest prize, not by employing physical power but by moral force and nonviolence. And he succeeded. It took courage, creativity, going to prison, being beaten, suffering, and sacrifice. As they watched this little man—how he lived and what he was willing to endure for them—the people of India came to trust him and to follow him. The people of England came to respect him and to believe that he was right. And what was impossible to imagine came to pass.

A journalist once asked Gandhi, "What is your message to the world?" It was his answer that transfixed me. It was written on the wall of the museum where Gandhi was assassinated. When I read his words, for a full minute, I could not move. I stood there captivated, contemplating what he said.

"What is your message to the world?" the reporter asked. Gandhi replied, "My life is my message."

On just about anyone else's lips, those words would sound arrogant. But coming from this humble man, they were inspiring and compelling. They had the ring of authenticity, so much so that when I read them, I stood transfixed, unable to move.

There is power when a person's life lines up with his words. When someone's message matters and when his life is the embodiment of that message, there is power in that person's life. It is the power of authenticity. It is an authority that cannot be ignored. It is a life that will ring out around the world and down through history. Even for eternity.

Gandhi's life was his message. "I believe in justice. I believe in freedom. I believe in compassion. I believe in loving my enemies."

Gandhi's life was his message, and his message was his life. So is yours. What do you want your life to say? What do you believe in so much that you want your life to proclaim it? Who or what do you care about so deeply that you must speak it and you must live it and you must make it the priority of your existence?

I believe there is a place within your being where your gifts and your abilities and your concerns come together. That is your message for the world. That is God's calling on your life. That is the gift you have to give to the world.

It's in your heart. Often we preachers try to get people to do something good that needs doing "out there," either out in the church or out in society. But that's wrong. We should instead tell you to do something great that's "in here"—inside your heart. We should tell you to do something that must be done and must be done by you because God put it there and he's counting on you to bring it into the world.

I want you to contemplate two ways of living. Which of them will bring you more joy?

In one life, you try to be a good person. You say "yes" when you are asked to help. You make being happy your life's goal. You stay busy, always trying to do more, achieve more, and have more. Can you see it—all that such a life might be?

In the second life, you live a different way. You have discovered your God-given purpose. You see yourself as God sees you: forgiven and accepted in Christ; gifted and empowered by the Spirit. In this life you have overcome your fears and your insecurities. You know who you are, why you're here, and what you are to do with your life. You are able to stand before the world, confident and certain of your calling, afraid of nothing but failing God. Imagine this life for yourself. Can you see it—who you could be, what you might do, the joy that you would experience?

That's who you are meant to be. That's the life you were created to live. You are here to say something important. Your life is meant to birth something unique and powerful into the world.

Imagine yourself being the person God created you to be. See yourself fulfilling his purpose for your life. And let yourself feel the joy you would know.

There are two lives you can live. One is a life of busyness; the other is a life of purposefulness. One is a life obsessed with being happy; the other is a life intent on serving others. One is the way of the world; the other is the way of Jesus.

Which life will bring you joy? Choose that life.

5

GUILT

If we claim to be without sin, we deceive ourselves and the truth is not in us. If we confess our sins, he is faithful and just and will forgive us our sins and purify us from all unrighteousness.

(1 John 1:8-9)

I first met John when he stepped into my office. He was the owner of a very successful manufacturing business. He lived in a beautiful home in a gated community that looked out on a lake. Outwardly, he seemed to "have it all." But his inner life was a very different story.

For several months, John had been meeting weekly with a counselor I knew. He had been struggling with depression and other emotional problems. Working with the counselor had been helpful. Together they had made some real progress in helping John get to a better place. But the counselor knew he had some other issues, deeper issues. He told John, "You need to deal with your spiritual life. You need to meet with a pastor."

It was a Saturday morning when John and I met for the first time. He sat down and after a few minutes began to tell me about his life. He was very open and honest about the mistakes he had made and the harm his selfishness had brought upon others. With tears in his eyes, he told me how deeply he regretted what he had done. Unable to look at me, he said, "I detest the man that I've become."

I'll never forget what John said next. "Do you know how hard it is to shave when you can't look at yourself in the mirror?" he asked. "For the past year and a half, not once have I looked in the mirror when I was shaving because I can't stand to look at myself. I'm so disappointed. I'm so disgusted with the man I have become."

John had a problem. His conscience filled him with overwhelming guilt. You have a similar problem. Odds are it isn't as striking or as debilitating as John's, but you have a problem like his. You have a conscience. The reason having a conscience is a problem is that sometimes you do what you shouldn't do. At other times, you don't do what you should. When you do something contrary to what you should, you have a conscience that makes you feel guilty. Guilt makes us feel unworthy. Over time it can destroy our self-esteem and make us feel alienated from God.

Even if our guilt is not as overwhelming as John's was, it is always unpleasant and painful. It robs us of our peace of mind and it steals our joy.

In his classic introduction to faith, *Mere Christianity*, C. S. Lewis writes that there are two odd facts about human beings. The first is that we believe in right and wrong. We all think there is a sort of behavior we ought to practice. You can call it fair play or common decency or morality. We may define it differently, but all of us believe there are certain behaviors that are right and certain behaviors that are wrong.

Lewis's second odd fact about human beings is that very often instead of doing what's right, we do what's wrong—not just what others say is wrong, but what we ourselves believe to be wrong. In addition, we often fail to do what we deem to be right, decent, and honorable. Humans are odd, Lewis writes, because we believe in right and wrong, yet we don't always choose what we know to be right.[1]

Human beings have been aware of this disparity between their beliefs and their actions since the beginning of time. Adam and Eve ate the forbidden fruit, and they began to hide from God. Why? Because they felt guilty (Genesis 3:1-13). Paul described this discrepancy between beliefs and actions when he wrote, "I do not understand what I do. For what I want to do I do not do, but what I hate I do" (Romans 7:15). We see it in more recent literature as well. Shakespeare's Lady Macbeth is tormented and driven to madness, unable to rid her conscience of her guilt in the death of Duncan. Edgar Allen Poe's protagonist goes insane in "The Tell-Tale Heart" because of a guilty conscience that drives him mad.

Thousands of years apart, coming from different cultures, the message is the same: We have a problem, and that problem is guilt. When we do wrong, we feel not just that we have violated some standard of right and wrong, but we feel as if we have violated ourselves. The results are often guilt and shame; and there may be nothing more painful that human beings must bear.

How do we escape the joy stealer of guilt? One way would be to live a perfect life, never making another moral mistake for the rest of our lives. Call me negative, but I'm thinking that's not going to be our way out. Unless people are already confusing you as "the other only-begotten Son of God," chances are moral perfection is not a real option for you to avoid guilt in the future.

What can we do, then, to overcome the feelings of self-condemnation and loathing that come from feeling guilty? Is there some other way? There is. In fact, there are four methods that people have found very helpful in overcoming the shame and the self-loathing that often robs us of the joy God intends us to know.

You may not "warm up" to all of these methods and I won't blame you if you don't. Fact is, there's only one of the four that I recommend, but they can all be found in the Bible. They have worked in the past for others, and they are working still. My guess is you may already be using them and possibly with great success.

1. Blame someone else.

The first technique is the oldest and most reliable ways of ridding ourselves of guilt that human beings have devised. In fact, it was developed in the garden of Eden. You remember the story. God placed Adam and Eve in a garden paradise. Everything was good. In fact, it was very good until they did the one thing God told them not to do. Eve ate from the one tree that God had said was off limits. Then she gave some of its forbidden fruit to Adam, and he was only too happy to do what God had told him not to do.

Next thing you know, God shows up and finds Adam and Eve hiding out of fear. And then the question they must have dreaded, "Have you eaten from the tree that I commanded you not to eat from?" (Genesis 3:11).

Denying what they had done would do no good. The evidence, no doubt, was everywhere to be seen: apple cores or orange peels or whatever it was, not to mention the feelings of guilt and shame that were causing them to hide. The proof was all over the ground and in their souls.

Adam realizes he's in real trouble when God asks him if he has eaten from the forbidden tree. He's about to lose everything good in his life. But then the light went on. "The man said, 'The woman you put here with me—she gave me some fruit from the tree, and I ate it'" (Genesis 3:12).

What a brilliant strategy! If you can't deny your guilt (and sad to say there will be times when you can't), you can always deny your responsibility. That's the first strategy you can employ for escaping a guilty conscience. Blame someone else.

Adam said: "The woman, God. It was the woman. I was just sitting here, minding my own business. I don't remember exactly what I was doing, but I was probably praying, and all of a sudden, this beautiful creature snuggles up beside me. She starts talking to me real sweet, and before I knew it I was eating this piece of fruit. Yes, I ate a little bit. But it wasn't my fault. Not really. If you want to get angry at someone, Lord, and I can understand if you do, fine. But don't get mad at me; get mad at the woman who tricked me."

Now, this method for avoiding guilt became very popular very quickly. In the very next verse we read, "Then the LORD God said to the woman, 'What is this you have done?' The woman said, 'The serpent deceived me, and I ate'" (Genesis 3:13).

In other words, the woman said: "It wasn't me, God. OK, it was me, but it wasn't my fault. I was just hanging around the tree. I had no plans of eating anything. And out of nowhere this serpent came up to me, and started asking me questions—'Did God really say this?' and 'Did God really say that?' and I got confused. Before I knew it, I ate some of the fruit. But it's not really my fault. I was tricked. I was deceived. I'm a victim more than a villain. If you want to punish someone, OK. But don't punish me; punish the snake."

Do you see how this method works? Earlier generations called it "passing the buck." Not long ago it was referred to as "the blame game." I think now it's so common in our culture you can call it "the American Way" for dealing with guilt.

Whatever name you give it, even though it was the first method developed, it still remains one of the most effective ways for stifling an accusatory conscience. It's a classic because it still works, and people continue to find it very helpful in getting rid of their guilt and shame.

If you can't deny what you've done, simply refuse to take responsibility for your actions. Blame someone else. "I know it was wrong, but he did it to me first." "I know it was wrong, but she had no right to talk to me like that." "I know I shouldn't have, but someone needed to take that arrogant jerk down a few notches."

If you work at it, you can almost always find some other person to blame for what you did and for the guilt you're feeling. And if you can't—if all else fails—you can always blame God. Look at Adam's answer again. "The man said, 'The woman you put here with me—she gave me some fruit from the tree, and I ate it'" (Genesis 3:12).

The woman *you* put here with me. "God, if we're talking guilt here, can we get real? I would have never eaten the fruit if YOU hadn't put the woman here to begin with. Lord, you should have known better. You know how beguiling she is and how weak I am. Honestly, I feel like you set me up just a little bit. Why did you put me in this situation in the first place?"

If you can't find someone else to blame, don't despair. Just blame God, he's always there.

"What I did may have been wrong, but things have been going so bad for me. I just gave in." Translation: "God, if you were looking out for me a little better, I wouldn't have acted that way."

"I know it wasn't right, but I've been so depressed and so lonely." Meaning: "God, if you would provide me with some friends, or if you had given me a spouse who was understanding, or if you would just get life to treat me fairly, then I wouldn't do the things I do."

"I know I shouldn't have done that, but I was so tired and drained." In other words: "God, you shouldn't make anyone live the way I have to live."

You don't actually have to say the words. There are lots of ways to communicate the attitude that, "God, you bear some responsibility for the mess I've made of things. If you were doing your part a little better, I would do my part better." Honestly, once you decide to go with this method, it's easy to blame God for all kinds of things. For some people, it becomes second nature. They do it so often and so deftly, they're not even aware of what they're doing.

You may have an objection to this strategy. You may be thinking, "If we deny our responsibility for our actions, we are denying our humanity. Isn't that what distinguishes us from the animal world? It's more than just being more intelligent, or walking upright, or having opposable thumbs, after all. What makes us human is that we know the difference between right and wrong, and we can make morally responsible decisions."

Well, aren't you the armchair philosopher! Look, if you object to this method, fine. Don't use it. There are three more you may like better. But since the beginning of time, blaming someone else has been very effective in helping people avoid the unpleasant feelings of guilt. It's just as popular today as it has ever been. In fact, for all your protesting, chances are you've already been using this method yourself to get rid of guilt.

Here's a second strategy that might work for you if you don't want to use the first.

2. Compare yourself to others.

Comparing yourself to others can be an effective way to diminish a guilty conscience. If you can stay busy looking at the shortcomings of others, you can almost always avoid looking at your own.

Jesus told a story about two men who went to the temple to pray. One was a tax collector. The other was a Pharisee. If anybody ever needed to find a way to overcome guilt, it was this poor tax collector. "The tax collector stood at a distance. He would not even look up to heaven, but beat his breast and said, 'God, have mercy on me, a sinner'" (Luke 18:13).

Now there's a man with a guilty conscience. He feels unworthy to look up at God. He's beating his chest. He's crying out for mercy and calls himself a sinner.

But look how cool the other man is. "The Pharisee stood by himself and prayed: 'God, I thank you that I am not like other people—robbers, evildoers, adulterers—or even like this tax collector. I fast twice a week and give a tenth of all I get'" (Luke 18:11-12).

Wow. Standing right there in the temple, in the very presence of God, and he doesn't even feel a twinge of conscience. What's his secret? Here it is, and it's a good one. Instead of comparing himself to the standards of God, he compared himself to the sins of others.

Sure, sure, if you read the Bible every now and then, you may feel the need to raise an objection. The man who escaped his conscience was a Pharisee, and Jesus frequently condemned the Pharisees as hypocrites. You might even want to quote the last verse of the parable, where Jesus says it was the tax collector, not the Pharisee, who went home right with God (Luke 18:14).

But let me ask you a question? Which of the two men do you think went home feeling more self-satisfied?

I have people come into my office who are striving to live for Christ, and they have tears in their eyes. They say, "I've accepted Jesus, and I'm trying to live for God. More than anything else, I want to yield all that I am to Christ. But still I sin. I feel like such a hypocrite." Does that sound like someone who's content and satisfied with themselves?

The best Christians I know sometimes feel like hypocrites. The best hypocrites I know never do.

The Pharisee in the parable felt great about himself. He never felt guilty or hypocritical. His conscience was always clear.

I can tell you how it's going to play out for the other man in the parable. Even though Jesus says he is "justified before God," this poor tax collector is going to go home, and he's going to blow it again. He's going to sin. He's going to feel guilty. And he's going to have to go back to the temple and ask for forgiveness all over again.

If you want to escape that pattern of having to confess again and again, one of the best things you can do is what the Pharisee did: compare yourself to someone else. If you do it right, you will almost always avoid the pain of guilt. Here are some hints for maximizing the benefit of this method.

First, compare yourself to people whose sins are more obvious than your own. Don't think of Billy Graham or Mother Teresa or even your saintly grandmother, for goodness' sake. Learn from the Pharisee in the story and compare yourself to someone whose sins are more public and more grievous than your own. "God, I thank you I'm not like robbers, evildoers, adulterers." Compare yourself to drug dealers, murderers, people who get caught cheating on their taxes, public figures accused of sexual harassment, folks who don't go to church, people who vote for the wrong political party because they don't have "Christian values." You're not like them, thank God. Make it easy on yourself. Lower the bar and always choose to compare yourself to others whose sins are easy to spot and to condemn.

Second, compare yourself to someone you don't know well. It's much easier to think the worst about people when you don't know the burdens they carry. If you're aware of how hard they've worked, how far they've traveled or how much they've had to overcome to get to where they are now—well, that can make it pretty difficult to feel superior to them.

Third, if you ever catch the other person doing something good, just tell yourself he's probably doing it for the wrong motive. She has something to gain financially. He wants to be seen by others. She's trying to make up for something wrong she did. Assuming the worst about "the competition" will always make you feel better about yourself.

Use these three little hints, and you can compare yourself to others with the full confidence that you will almost never be bothered with feelings of guilt. In fact, you'll probably end up feeling very good about yourself.

If you don't like this method, if it seems a bit too unbiblical or un-Christlike, there is a third way for getting rid of guilt. I'll admit right up front that this one is, well, a little drastic. Here it is.

3. Worship a false god.

Creating a false god to worship will clear your conscience right up. Before you think you could never use this one, let me explain it. Try to be open-minded and avoid a negative, knee-jerk reaction. This one really does work. I know it sounds extreme, but people do this all the time to avoid their guilt. Sure, "false" sounds a little idolatrous. I understand why you might not warm up to this one right away. Let me rephrase it. "Create a different picture of God, preferably one made in your own image." Or at least one that is "you-friendly." Why? Because it is much easier to please the gods we create than to satisfy the God who created us.

A "you-friendly" god is a god who's not bothered by the mistakes you most often make or the practices you don't want to give up. With a god like this, remade in your own image, you don't have to sweat that stuff. Your new god will be particularly impressed with the good that you do. What matters most to this god is not so much what you do or don't do, but just that your heart's in the right place. And heaven knows yours is, I'm sure.

So, for example, if you find it easy to love your neighbor, that really pleases your god and you get extra points. If you find it hard not to love your neighbor's spouse, well, that's not a "biggee" with a you-friendly god. So don't feel bad about it.

Again, this method for getting rid of guilt comes right out of the Bible. When the Israelites made their exodus out of Egypt, they came to the promised land of Canaan. The people who lived there, the Canaanites, were strange folks, and they had some bizarre practices. But one thing they didn't have was a problem with their consciences.

Their secret was creating a god in their own image. Two religious practices among some of the Canaanites involved, get this, feasting and fornicating in the presence of their idols. Now there's a you-friendly god, made in their own image. And very easy to please. Take two of our most basic, physical drives and elevate them to religious practices required by your god.

We, of course, are a little too sophisticated for a god as crass as that. But with just a little tinkering, even we can fashion a god who's pretty easy to get along with. If you want to go this route, just hold on to two thoughts. I call them "Mottoes for Modern-day Canaanites."

The first is "God knows I'm only human." Start there, and you are halfway home to reshaping a god who won't bother you with guilt.

Take the command, "Be holy because I, the LORD your God, am holy" (Leviticus 19:2) and then add, "but God knows I'm only human." Then the command gets turned into "Do the best you can and don't worry about the rest." Read where Jesus said, "Whoever wants to be my disciple must deny themselves and take up their cross and follow me" (Matthew 16:24), then simply add, "but God knows I'm only human." In your mind that radical command will sound very much like, "Believe in Jesus and try to be a good person."

Add this second motto for modern-day Canaanites, and you're home free: "God wants me to be happy." God loves me. And when I love people, I want them to be happy, so I'm sure God wants me to be happy.

Keep saying this motto to yourself, "God wants me to be happy, God wants me to be happy, God wants me to be happy." Pretty soon it will sound just like "God wants whatever makes me happy." So if something makes you happy, it will become very easy to believe that it's probably OK with God. And if something is making you unhappy—like being faithful to a spouse who can be difficult—it's probably not that important to God, anyway. Why? Because God wants you to be happy.

If you think this is hard to pull off, you're wrong. Several times in my ministry, I have had men talk with me about wanting to get out of their marriages. They say something like, "Rob, tell me what you think. I met a woman at work. She was really nice, and we started spending some time together. We never meant for anything to happen, but we have fallen in love. Probably because we have so much in common. I've been unhappy in my marriage, and it turns out she's been unhappy in her marriage. We've become intimate, and we really make each other happy. I think that just maybe God brought her into my life, and it's his will for us to get married because we're so good together. What do you think?"

Do I think God brought these people together? Do I think that instead of working on their own marriages, God wants them to break the vows they took at the altar and start cheating on their spouses? Heck no, I don't think God brought them together. And if I wasn't a preacher, I'd use a lot stronger word than "heck."

As I've said before, God's primary goal in your life is not to make you happy. It's to make you holy. That means turning away from temptation, asking forgiveness when we sin, and doing the hard work of restoring our relationships and becoming persons of integrity. There are times when that won't make us happy.

But, I digress. The point is not to tell you how to become holy with this method, but to show you how to avoid guilt and shame. And the way to do that is to recreate the God of the universe into a god made in your own image. With just these two mottoes— "God knows I'm only human" and "God wants me to be happy"— without much trouble, we can transform an awesome, holy God into a kindly grandfather figure. No matter what we do, this god will pat us on the head and smile.

Again, I know you may object to this method. You're familiar with the time God revealed himself to Moses, and he said that his name was "Yahweh," which translated means "I AM WHO I AM" (Exodus 3:14). You want to point out that God's name is not "I am who you want me to be," or "I am what you believe I should be," or "I am whoever you need me to be to feel good about yourself."

I understand you might be reluctant to employ this strategy. But I also know that people do it. They do it all the time. They reshape and refashion God until they can feel good about him and even better about themselves. I hear them do it when they say, "Well, the God I believe in . . ." and they fill in the blank with what they would or wouldn't ever do.

Criticize this method, if you must. But it sure seems effective in helping people live with themselves and avoid the pain of guilt. We live in an age of designer jeans, designer drugs, and designer gods. Our culture is all about options and finding what fits, what works for us. You can tell yourself you would never do that. Maybe you wouldn't. Maybe not consciously. Maybe not purposefully. Maybe not at all. Maybe never. Maybe.

So far, I've told you how to get rid of a guilty conscience by replacing it with an easy conscience. And if that's what you want, any of these methods will do. As they say in AA, "It works if you work it." Work at these three methods, and they'll work for you.

If you want something else, something more, you'll have to go with the last option. The other three can give you an easy conscience that can erase the feelings of guilt. But only this last one can give you a clean conscience that erases the sin that creates the feelings of guilt.

4. Get right with God.

Do you want an easy conscience or a clean conscience? Do you want your sins to be quieted or your sins to be forgiven? Do you wish for your guilty feelings to be relieved or for your guilt before God and within yourself to be removed? The first three methods of dealing with guilt I've discussed will help you get rid of guilty feelings, but only this last one will remove the guilt itself, the very reason for your uneasy conscience. If you desire to be cleansed of your sin and rid of the reason for your guilt, then you're ready to get right with God. But how do you do it?

First, be honest about what you have done. Being honest means we take responsibility for our actions. We don't minimize what we have done or blame our circumstances or what others have done to us.

This should be easy for us. The Bible is clear that "all have sinned and fall short" (Romans 3:23). "All" includes us, so it shouldn't come as a surprise to us when we sin. We hope and pray and open our lives to the transforming work of the Spirit so that we will grow in grace and sin less often and less grievously. But "if we claim to be without sin, we deceive ourselves and the truth is not in us" (1 John 1:8).

Even the apostle Paul admitted, "Not that I have already obtained this or have already reached the goal; but I press on to make it my own, because Christ Jesus has made me his own" (Philippians 3:12 NRSV). Paul is saying that he is still a work in progress. So are we, and we will be all our lives. "Works in progress" fail and make mistakes. "Works in progress" stumble and sin. So, admitting our sin and taking responsibility for our actions should be easy. But often it's not. Our pride gets in the way. It's our nature to trust in our own goodness, rather than in the grace of God, for a sense of being acceptable and worthy of love. We try to protect our sense of "being a good person," so we are always tempted to deny the wrong we have done, minimize the depravity of our deeds, or make excuses for our actions. But we can never experience freedom from guilt and the forgiveness of our sin when we refuse to be honest with ourselves and with God about what we have done.

Let me say briefly that sometimes people struggle with "false guilt." It's possible to feel guilty when you're not actually guilty. A mistake in judgment is not a sin. Sometimes you want to do right and you try to do right, but you misunderstand the situation and your words or your actions made the situation worse. That can be embarrassing, and you should learn from your mistake about making certain you know what's going on before you speak or act. You might even need to apologize to another person if you hurt them in some way. But a mistake in judgment is not sinful, and you don't need to feel guilty or ask for forgiveness from God. Simply ask for wisdom for the future.

There are other examples of false guilt. For instance, some of us grew up being shamed for our feelings or for our opinions or for speaking up for ourselves. Later in life, when you say what you think and it bothers other people, because of your past, you may start to feel guilty, even ashamed, for speaking up. Don't do that. You have a voice. You have a right to express your feelings. Just because someone doesn't like what you said or did, that doesn't mean you were wrong. Examine why you feel guilty. If your motive was pure and your words were not demeaning, what you are feeling is "false guilt." You don't need to ask for forgiveness. You need to overcome the wrong, shaming messages that lead you to feel this way and acknowledge your self-worth.

But there are times, too many times, when our feelings of guilt are well deserved. We have done wrong. In those moments, we need to be honest with ourselves and with God—and that means accepting responsibility for what we have done.

Next, confess your sin to God. John tells us, "If we confess our sins, he is faithful and just and will forgive us our sins" (1 John 1:9). Our English word *confess* comes from two Latin words, one meaning "with" and the other "to declare." The Greek word in 1 John 1:9 that is translated as "confess" has a similar meaning. It could literally be translated as "to say the same thing."

When we confess our sins, we are saying the same thing as— we are agreeing with—God about our sin. That's why Augustine wrote, "he who confesses his sins already acts with God."[2]

This verse is wonderful news and rich in meaning. It shows us that what is required for forgiveness is simple confession. It says that forgiveness doesn't require acts of contrition or emotional self-flagellation. Simple confession is sufficient. Agreeing with God that what we did was wrong, in fact sinful, and asking for forgiveness is all that is required. We admit to God that we broke his law, that we offended his holiness, and that we rebelled against his rightful authority over our lives. We agree with God that we sinned and that our sin is grievous. (All sin is.) And we ask for forgiveness.

We trust in God's grace and mercy to remove our sins and make us right with himself. We don't trust in how badly we feel about our sins or how ardently we promise to do better in the future. We trust in God's grace—nothing else and nothing more.

The promise in this verse is that if we confess our sins, God will forgive us. Why? "Because he is faithful and just." It is "faithful" for God to forgive us when we ask for forgiveness because Jesus has made atonement for our sin. He has already paid our debt, the debt we could not pay, when he died on the cross for us. When God forgives us, he is being faithful to his Son. When we ask for forgiveness, God will honor what Jesus has done for us—he will be faithful to the sacrifice Christ made to cleanse us and free us from our guilt.

In a similar way, it is "just" for God to forgive us because our debt has already been paid in Christ. It would be unjust to require that our debt be paid twice—once by Jesus and then another time by us.

We can be confident when we ask for forgiveness because our forgiveness is based on the character of God—his faithfulness and his justice. But you may be thinking, *It can't be as easy as I just confess and all my guilt is taken away.*

I didn't say it was easy. It was awful. It was horrendous. It was Jesus being spat upon. It was Jesus having his back torn apart with a whip. It was Jesus having spikes driven through his wrists and his ankles. It was Jesus being stripped naked and listening to men mock him and call him a fool. It was Jesus on a cross, the blood weeping out of his body, and his spirit crying, "My God, my God, why have you forsaken me?" (Mark 15:34). It was the Father watching his Son be tortured and crucified, hearing his Son cry out his name, and allowing him to die on the cross so we could be forgiven.

Easy? Nothing could have been harder. But it was done so we could be forgiven, freed from the burden of guilt, and restored to a right relationship with God. Sometimes people are able to believe that God has forgiven them, but they cannot—or will not—forgive themselves. I think they are under the misimpression that if they let go of their guilt, it means they don't take what they have done seriously. Or it may be that they feel unworthy of joy, so they continue to hold on to their guilt.

In seminary, we were required to spend some time doing "field ed." Some of us ministered in hospitals or in churches. I spent one year in a church, a little "start-up" in one of Boston's urban neighborhoods where 80 percent of the people who attended were alcoholics, ex-convicts, or patients who had been released from mental institutions.

Another year I spent working in a prison. The most joyful, likeable Christian there was a huge man named Alfredo. He was six feet four and weighed 280 pounds, all muscle. He was always smiling. Alfredo had killed a man. But he had accepted Christ, experienced the grace of God, and he was a new man.

Alfredo was a leader whose influence on others was as big as he was. He encouraged others in that prison to be faithful to Christ and grow in their faith. He had led many others who were as guilty as he was into the same kind of life-transforming relationship with Jesus that he had.

There was another man in the prison I came to know well. His name was Freddy, and he, too, had killed a man. And he had accepted Christ. But unlike Alfredo, Freddy rarely came out of his cell. All day and night, he was on his bunk, with the light usually off. He lived in darkness, unhappy and morose.

Why was there such a difference between the two men who had committed the same crime, lived in the same place, and had accepted the same Savior? Alfredo had forgiven himself, but Freddy never could. There is one other difference between them. Alfredo was used powerfully by God in the lives of others. Freddy was no encouragement to others, and he never led anyone to Christ.

Which of these two men honored Christ more? Was it the one who continued to live with guilt and shame, trying to prove how sorry he was for what he had done? Or was it the one who trusted Jesus that he had been forgiven, internalized it within his spirit, and lived with great joy as a new creation in Christ?

If you have confessed your sins, you have been forgiven. You do not please God by feeling or acting like you're still guilty. You have been set free; you do not honor God by living like a slave. If you have been made into a new creation in Christ, you do not glorify God by walking around like you're the same creature you were before you were born again. Jesus did not die on the cross so you would feel guilty; he died on the cross so you could feel forgiven.

Listen. You are not who your past says you are. You are not who your parents or others from your past said you are. You are not who your sins say you are. You are not who the accuser says you are. You are who God says you are. And he says that in Christ you are forgiven, accepted, and loved.

Whatever you have done that makes you feel guilty and unworthy of joy, you're not the only one who has done it. God has seen it before. God has been forgiving people from the beginning of time. Whatever you've done, he's forgiven it before. Whatever you have become, he has loved it before. And wherever you are, he's right there with you with his arms open to receive you.

Confess your sin. Trust that God is faithful and just and will forgive your sin. And then live that way. Live that way until you feel that way. Live as someone forgiven, free, grateful, and full of joy.

There's something else you may need to do if you haven't already been freed of your guilt.

Accept Jesus Christ as your Savior and Lord. In Romans 3:21-25 Paul writes: "God has shown us a way to be made right with him. . . . We are made right with God by placing our faith in Jesus Christ. . . . For God presented Jesus as the sacrifice for sin. People are made right with God when they believe that Jesus sacrificed his life, shedding his blood" (NLT).

When we place our faith in Jesus Christ, we give up the illusion that we can make ourselves right with God. We let go of the false belief that we can do enough or be enough to make up for our sins. We accept the reality that we cannot save ourselves.

When we believe and place our trust in Christ, we come to the awful, wonderful realization that being religious won't save us, being moral won't save us, and being better than others won't save us. We take the bold step of trusting in God's grace, not our goodness; in his mercy, not our merit; in the sacrifice Christ made for us, not the sacrifices we might make for him.

When we do so, we receive the promise that when we do, God will remember our sins no more (Jeremiah 31:34), he will remove our transgressions from us as far as the east is from the west (Psalm 103:12), and he will cleanse us of our guilt (1 John 1:9).

A good friend of mine in high school was always a little wilder than I was. I joked that I didn't have to get into trouble, since I could just tell Marshall's stories and have the fun of living through him vicariously.

Marshall and I went to the same church growing up, and then we stayed in contact when we went to different colleges. I became involved in a Christian group on campus and grew in my faith. Marshall didn't. In fact, his "wild side," far from home, took on wings, and he embraced the party life. Charming and handsome, he slept with many women (whom he'd later say that he used), took lots of drugs, and often drank to excess. He walked away from the faith he had been taught in church, though there was always the thought lurking in the back of his mind that what he was doing was wrong—that he was guilty and needed to change.

A good friend of his at school was a committed Christian. Tommy loved Marshall as much as I did. And he could see the struggle within him—enticed by sin and yet feeling tormented by the way he was living.

One day after a game of basketball in the hot Texas sun, they went to the locker room to take a shower. They covered themselves with soap and stood under the hot water as it fell over them and washed the dirt and the sweat and the stench off their bodies.

They picked up warm, terry-cloth towels and began to dry off. "Marshall," Tommy whispered. "What?" Marshall responded, not looking up. Again Tommy, whispered, "Marshall." "What?" This time louder, "Marshall!" "What is it?" Marshall said, turning to see Terry holding the white towel to his face. Terry breathed in deeply and slowly. Then he said, "Marshall, it sure feels good to be clean."

It sure feels good to be clean—to know that you have been forgiven, to have a new start in life. That's why Jesus came. He came so your sins could be washed away and you could know what it's like to be a child of God—accepted, cleansed, and loved.

If you have never accepted Jesus as your Savior; if you have trusted in your own righteousness; or if you have believed you were beyond being forgiven, why not receive him now?

God has shown us a way of becoming right with him. It's admitting our sins, acknowledging that we can never save ourselves, and believing that Jesus has paid the debt that we could never pay.

Finally, make amends to whomever you have harmed. This is not a requirement for receiving forgiveness, but it is an appropriate response to the forgiveness we have received. In other words, we don't make amends to earn salvation, but as a response to our salvation. Seeking to become right with others is one of the ways we honor Christ with the new life he has given us, and this frees us of the power of guilt.

Jesus taught: "If you are offering your gift at the altar and there remember that your brother or sister has something against you, leave your gift there in front of the altar. First go and be reconciled to them; then come and offer your gift" (Matthew 5:23-24).

Making amends means acknowledging to ourselves and to another person what we did. In some cases, it may be as simple as an apology. But usually it requires more.

It may mean paying a debt. If it's money we owe, we pay back our financial debt. If we damaged someone's reputation, we do all we can to restore it. If our selfishness created emotional damage within another person, we let that person know that we were wrong and he or she was right; and if there's a way to help with their healing, we offer to do that.

Making amends may mean living a different way. If we were unfaithful, we become faithful, attentive, and caring. If we were demeaning to another person, we become that person's encourager.

Paul tells us to "let no debt remain outstanding, except the continuing debt to love one another, for whoever loves others has fulfilled the law" (Romans 13:8). It may not be easy to make amends. Sometimes doing so requires courage. It almost always requires humility. But it brings joy to know that we have done all we can to repair the wreckage we have created in the lives of others. The sooner we learn to take responsibility for our actions and make amends to the people we have harmed, the better our lives and the lives of those around us will be.

There is no greater joy in life than knowing that you are right with God, that you are right with yourself, and you have done all you can to be right with others.

John was still looking down when he spoke the last words of his confession to me that Saturday morning in my office. "For the past year and a half, not once have I looked in the mirror when I was shaving because I can't stand to look at myself. I'm so disappointed. I'm so disgusted with the man I have become."

I asked him to look at me and I told him, "The Bible says that Jesus came into the world for people like you. And we're going to find out if this God thing is true, right here, right now. You're going to get on your knees and confess your sins to God. I'm going to be on my knees right next to you, and I'm going to put my hand on your shoulder. And when you have finished praying, I'm going to ask God to make it real to you that Jesus Christ died for you and that his death covers every sin you have ever committed. I am going to pray that the Holy Spirit will come into your heart and release you from guilt and shame and that before you stand up, you will know that God loves you."

That's what we did. And that is exactly what happened. As he prayed, John's tears began to flow. But somewhere in the middle of our prayers, his tears changed from tears of shame and regret into tears of joy. The Spirit of God embraced him, and he left my office a new man. He was released from the weight of his sin, and he was freed of the guilt that had paralyzed him and stolen his joy. It's been years now, and he is still free.

You have a problem. You have a conscience, and you don't always do what you should. And the result is guilt.

You have a Savior. He came for people like you and me, people who do wrong and who need grace. He came for people who are going to be a work in progress as long as we live. He came so we could be forgiven. Don't wait. Trust in his grace today, and know the joy of being set free.

6

THE SECRET TO LIVING WITH JOY

I know what it is to be in need, and I know what it is to have plenty. I have learned the secret of being content in any and every situation, whether well fed or hungry, whether living in plenty or in want. I can do all this through him who gives me strength.

(Philippians 4:12-13)

Up to this point, we have seen how worry, bitterness, negativity, busyness, and guilt can rob us of the joy God desires us to experience. We have also looked at the positive steps we can take to overcome these joy stealers and experience the abundant life offered to us in Jesus Christ. But there's more to the joy-filled life than overcoming self-defeating attitudes and actions. We must adopt a proactive, positive approach to life if we are to know the deep, abiding joy promised to us in the gospel.

No one, other than Jesus, models the positive steps that lead to a joy-filled life as much as does the apostle Paul. That's an amazing statement when you realize that Paul was ostracized by his friends, persecuted by his enemies, subjected to immense physical suffering, and constantly burdened by his concern for the young (and often troubled) churches he had planted. If we can learn the lessons Paul has to teach us, then maybe we, too, even in the most negative of circumstances, can experience great joy.

Nearly two thousand years ago in his letter to the Philippians, Paul wrote: "I have learned the secret of being content in any and every situation . . ." (Philippians 4:12). I appreciate Paul's honesty in this passage. He tells the Philippians that he has "learned" to be content. Being at peace and living with joy was not Paul's natural condition. He wasn't an optimistic, glass-is-half-full kind of guy by disposition. It wasn't his natural predisposition before he met Jesus on the Damascus road. It wasn't even his normal state after he came to faith in Christ. He had to learn to be content.

Paul wrote that he had learned to be content "in any and every situation." If there was ever a guy who had a penchant for getting into any and every situation, it was Paul. Five times he was given thirty-nine lashes. Three times he was beaten with rods. Three times he was shipwrecked. Once he was stoned by an angry mob. On many occasions he went without food and water (2 Corinthians 11:21-29). In fact, when he wrote to the Philippians, Paul was in prison, waiting to stand trial, knowing that he could very well be sentenced to death. And to make matters even worse, most of the people he has counted on in the past had deserted him.

There in prison Paul wrote his letter to the church in Philippi. Four little chapters. But today, twenty centuries later, commentators often refer to this letter as Paul's epistle of joy. Fifteen times in these four short chapters, Paul writes about his joy or calls upon the Philippians to rejoice.

When I read Paul's words about learning the secret of being content in any situation, I have two reactions. The first one is, I become excited. If Paul could learn to be content, it means so can I. So can you. Even if we're not optimistic by nature, even if our circumstances are difficult, even if it seems like the whole world is against us, Paul's words and his example tell us that we can be at peace and live with joy. That's great news. All we need to do is learn the secret that Paul discovered.

My second reaction is very different. I get frustrated. Why? Because nowhere in his letter to the Philippians does Paul tell us what the secret is.

I want to say, "Paul, brother, come on, please! You've got what I need. You've got what the world is crying out for. Give it to us, just as plain as you can. Write a book. Title it 'Joy for Dummies,' and you'll have a best seller."

Paul doesn't tell us his secret for joy—at least, not in so many words. But if we look at what he wrote to the believers in Philippi, I think we can come pretty close to Paul's formula for being at peace and living with joy no matter what is going on around us.

1. We must get our expectations right, and the right expectation is that life will be hard.

If you want to be happy, I think Paul would tell you, expect life to be a struggle. Somehow we've gotten it into our heads that if we're having problems, we must be doing something wrong or someone else must be doing something wrong to us. Our subconscious assumption is that life is supposed to run smoothly. It's supposed to follow the schedule we've set for it and work itself out according to our predetermined plans. If life's not doing that, then something must be wrong.

What's wrong is our expectation that life should be and will be easy. Most people will tell you they don't believe that, but when life gets hard, listen to them. They cry out with great sincerity and emotion, "Why is this happening to me? What have I done to deserve this? Why is—fill in the blank: my job, my marriage, raising kids, being happy, doing the right thing—so hard?"

Why is life hard? There are many reasons.

For one thing, you're a physical being. Over time all things physical break down, wear out, and stop working. When that physical thing that breaks down, wears out, and stops working is you, it makes life hard.

You're also connected to other people. Your relationships with others will bring you immense joy and be your greatest blessing. But they will also bring you pain and break your heart. Your friends will fail you, and that hurts. Your enemies will attack you, and that hurts. People you've helped will forget you. People who don't know you will hear and believe the worst about you. The people you love will suffer physically and emotionally. Try as you might, there will be times when you cannot take away their pain or make their lives better. In those terrible moments, you will feel helpless and have to watch them suffer. And because you care, your life will be hard.

Another thing that makes life hard is that you are a difficult person. Anyone ever tell you that? Well, you are, and it's time someone told you. You're a difficult person. What I mean is that you sometimes make life more difficult for yourself than it has to be. You worry about things you don't need to worry about. You feel guilty when you don't need to feel that way. You refuse to address problems that would go away if you would just face them. You act before you think. You get angry about things that don't matter. You think the world is out to get you when it's not. And you get your feelings hurt over things you should just laugh off.

In other words, you are a mess. And nobody makes life as hard for you as you do. OK, I don't know for sure that this is true about you, but I'm guessing it's true for you since I know it's true for me. I don't remember where I read the following quotation, but it's one of my favorites. "Coping with a difficult person is always a problem, especially when the difficult person happens to be you." I am a difficult person, and it makes my life hard. And odds are, the same is true for you.

Just to make certain you don't miss it, I'll say it again. You are a difficult person and that makes life hard.

What's more, you live in a world that's unfair. You and I live in a world where bad things happen to good people. Whether it's by accident or by the evil intentions of others, you and the people you love will suffer the pain of unfairness during your lifetime.

Life for all human beings is unpredictable, uncontrollable, and full of problems. Expect life to be hard. Expect marriage to be hard. Expect parenting to be hard. Expect truly loving another person to be hard. Expect growing old to be hard.

When you are cheated, overlooked, or mistreated; when you hurt and those you love are suffering; when life is unfair, do not feel like you've been singled out. Don't feel like life or God owes you an explanation. You're a human being, and human existence is hard. It's a struggle. It always has been, and it always will be.

Why do I think Paul would tell us to expect life to be difficult? Because in all of his writings, we don't find one word of self-pity. There's not one instance where he cries out, "Life's not fair; I deserve better than this." In prison for preaching the gospel, Paul doesn't write, "God, why do you allow me to be whipped and beaten? Why do you let me go hungry and cold when all I'm trying to do is be faithful?" Instead we read, "It has been granted to you on behalf of Christ not only to believe in him, but also to suffer for him, since you are going through the same struggle you saw I had" (Philippians 1:29-30).

Life is hard. Expect it to be that way. And when you decide that you will follow Jesus, you can expect it to be an even greater struggle. Decide that there's a higher calling on your life than being liked by others and becoming affluent, and you'll start swimming against the tide of how others think and act. Commit yourself to living for Christ in a world that lives for self, and the world will feel threatened and become more likely to attack you.

Determine to live for your principles in a world that will sell its soul for pleasure, and you can expect to be misunderstood, mistreated, and maligned. And if you want to live with joy, you had better expect life to be the way it is—not the way you wish it was or think it should be.

Life is difficult for everyone. That doesn't mean it can't be good. But if we expect it to be easy, we're more likely to live with disappointment and anger rather than contentment and joy.

2. We must get our focus right.

Here are two key insights for achieving peace and contentment. First, you can control your thought life. Second, you must control your thought life.

If you want to be miserable, that's easy. Simply dredge up the things that make you unhappy. Think about them, revisit them, allow yourself to become fixated on them. Chew on them over and over like a cow with its cud. As you do, tell yourself that you can't do otherwise. The problems and the fears and the hurts you're thinking about are so big, so important, so hurtful that you simply must think about them. It's just impossible to let them go.

Obsess about things in the past that went wrong, things in the present that are going wrong, things in the future that could go wrong. What someone said or did to you or someone you loved. Something someone should have done for you.

Focus on everything that's wrong, and you'll never feel right. Fixate on all that's bad, and you'll never feel good. But if you want to be content and live with joy, you'll need to control your thought life. John Milton described this reality in *Paradise Lost*. "The mind is its own place, and in it self / Can make a Heav'n of Hell, a Hell of Heav'n."[1]

One of my parishioners, a young mother in her thirties, made an appointment to see me. She was unhappy with her life. She detailed all the things she wished were different. She concluded by saying, "I just wished I had the life that Joan has."

Of course she wished she had Joan's life. Just about anyone would. Joan had married into a wealthy family to an easygoing man who was respected by everyone who knew him. She had a dream home on a hundred acres of land. She wore the finest clothes and was physically attractive. Her children were grown and successful. They lived close enough for her that she could see her grandchildren as often as she desired. She had it all. "I just wish I had the life that Joan has," said the young woman in my office. "Then I'd be happy." She would have been surprised had I told her that Joan's husband had sat in the same chair she was sitting in just two weeks earlier. He had come to see me because nothing in the world made Joan happy.

"She's just miserable, all the time," he told me. "Nothing is ever good enough for her. She always finds something wrong with everything—even with the kids. It's like she's looking for reasons to be unhappy. I've tried everything," her husband said. "I want to help her but I don't know how." He ended by saying, "Rob, if it wasn't for my commitment to Christ, I'd be here telling you that I was getting a divorce."

After counseling with literally hundreds of persons and couples, I've learned that it's not the people with the fewest problems who have the most joy. And it's not the people with the most blessings who experience the greatest happiness. The people who are most content are the ones who focus on what's good in their lives and who refuse to look for and fixate on the negatives. As the Swedish proverb states: "Those who wish to sing always find a song."

Paul instructed the Philippians, "Whatever is true, whatever is noble, whatever is right, whatever is pure, whatever is lovely, whatever is admirable—if anything is excellent or praiseworthy— think about such things" (Philippians 4:8).

It may sound like trite advice, but you'd be surprised how many people need to hear it. If you want to live full of joy, you will need to fill your mind with the thoughts that bring joy.

The following saying has been attributed to many different sources, including Ralph Waldo Emerson: "Sow a thought, reap an action; sow an act, reap a habit; sow a habit, reap a character; sow a character, reap a destiny."

Where does it begin? With sowing a thought. It doesn't begin just with having a thought, but with *planting* it within our minds where it can take root and grow. We do that by focusing on it, each time pushing it deeper and deeper into our psyche.

One of the glories of being a human being is that we are thoughtful, rational beings. That means how we think and what we think about will impact our lives. Consequently, one of the greatest and most important battles we will ever fight is the battle to control our thought life.

Lewis Thomas writes about a strange phenomenon that occurs in the Bay of Naples. A common sea slug, the nudibranch, produces larvae that often become caught in the tentacles of a medusa jellyfish. Eventually they are ingested by the medusa. Once inside the jellyfish, the little snails go to work. They start to eat. Over time, from the inside out, they begin to consume the jellyfish that consumed them, growing larger and devouring more all the time, until their work is finished and the medusa is no more.[2]

There's a lesson there, don't you think? Be careful what you consume because it will consume you. Be alert to the thoughts you put into your mind because once there they take on a life of their own and shape us and form—or deform—us.

If we fill our minds with thoughts that are critical and mean and unhealthy, they will consume us. Before long, we will be critical and mean and unhealthy. If, instead, we fill our minds with thoughts that are pure and beautiful and good, over time our hearts will become reservoirs of purity and beauty and goodness, and our lives will come to reflect the values of the kingdom of God and the image of Jesus. And the result will be joy.

If you want to be unhappy in your marriage, look for what's wrong with your spouse. You'll find something. Then think about it over and over. You will make yourself miserable, and you will ruin your marriage.

Concentrate on what's wrong with your children, your job, your church, the people you meet, the place you live. Fixate on what's wrong with yourself. In no time, you'll become dissatisfied, depressed, and defeated.

Or you can focus your mind on what's good in your spouse, your children, your job, your church, the people you meet, and the place you live. If that's what you're looking for, that's what you'll find. In the process, you will discover how blessed you are and how happy you can be.

When we are depressed, thinking good, positive, faith-filled thoughts is particularly difficult. It takes work and energy to take the high road mentally. It's always easy to go low. When we feel sorry for ourselves, it's especially difficult to think about what's good and positive and worthy of praise in our situation. But it's when we're down that it's especially important that we look up and focus on how God has blessed us. It's when we are weak and depressed that it's critical for us to fill our minds with the promises of God. It's then that we need to take the focus off of what's wrong and fix our minds on what's good and right in our lives.

There is so much of life you cannot control. You cannot control whether life is fair to you, whether people like you, or whether the economy and the stock market will rise or fall. You cannot control drunk drivers or cancer. There comes a point when you cannot control your children and the decisions they make. But the one thing in life you have absolute control over is the one thing in life that's most important: how you think and where you put your focus. You can decide what goals to pursue and how you invest your time and your energy. Being able to control your thought life is a great gift and a terrible responsibility that God has given you.

Even when life is challenging and unpleasant, claim that gift. Decide that you will control your thought life. It may be a challenge. You may have a lifelong pattern of looking for the negative in every situation. But you can teach yourself to think differently and to exercise your God-given ability to find and focus on what's good in your life. If you want to live with joy, you must.

3. We must get our attitude right.

I'm not a positive person by nature. I try to be. I try to see the opportunities instead of the obstacles. I do my best to emphasize the possibilities instead of the problems. But I'm a firstborn child, meaning I tend to feel responsible for everything. I'm also a perfectionist, which means I can find something wrong with just about everything. The combination is not a formula for a positive, optimistic outlook on life.

The truth is that depression and anxiety run in my family. It's something I have to fight all the time. So, I have to work on my attitude if it's going to help me instead of hurt me.

What did Paul tell the Philippians? "Do not be anxious about anything, but in every situation, by prayer and petition, with thanksgiving, present your requests to God" (Philippians 4:6).

Paul's admonition contains a wonderful insight. We don't have to be anxious because our circumstances are difficult or disappointing. With faith and the right attitude, the world "out there" won't control the world "in here" within our souls.

Maybe the greatest hindrance to happiness is the idea that something "out there" will make me content. There's something I don't have, something I want, something that others possess—if I just had that, then I'd be happy.

People who struggle to experience joy often suffer from one of the following maladies that I heard John Maxwell describe twenty-five years ago.[3]

"Destination Disease." This is the belief that someday when something happens, then I'll be happy. People with "destination disease" think thoughts like: "When we move to a larger house, when I get a new job, when I can buy a better car, when I get promoted, when I lose some weight, when I retire—then I'll be content."

"*Someone Sickness.*" This is the belief that my unhappiness is caused by somebody else who is or who isn't in my life. "When my boss is no longer a jerk, then I'll be happy." "When I get married, then I'll be happy." After we're married, it's "when the person I'm married to changes, then I'll be happy." "When my child's life is straightened out, when my spouse quits drinking, then I'll be able to enjoy life."

"*The Backward Blues.*" You could also call this one "If Only Illness." People who suffer from this malady blame their unhappiness on something that happened in the past. They keep looking backward, telling themselves, "If only that hadn't happened, I could be happy." "If only I hadn't taken that job, if only I hadn't made that investment, if only my sister hadn't stolen my boyfriend, if only my husband hadn't cheated on me, if only my parents had been proud of me," then I'd be happy.

The movie *Napoleon Dynamite* (2004) is the story of a group of misfits who are trying to find their way in life. The main character, Napoleon, is determined to make something of himself for many reasons, one of which is not wanting to turn out like his uncle Rico, whose life is going nowhere.

In one scene, Rico bemoans his life and how it all went badly because his high school coach did not put him in to play quarterback in the fourth quarter of an important game. If he had, Rico is sure "we'd have been state champions. No doubt. No doubt in my mind. You better believe things would've been different. I'd a gone pro in a heartbeat. I'd be making millions of dollars and living in a big ol' mansion somewhere. You know, soaking it up in a hot tub with my soul mate." Then with a wistful look he says to his nerdy nephew, "Kip, I reckon you know a lot about cyberspace. You ever come across anything like time travel?"

Uncle Rico suffers from the "backward blues." Whether it's a mistake we made that we regret, something hurtful that someone did to us, or an unfortunate event that happened long ago, "If Only Illness" tells us that something in the past is keeping us from being happy in the present.

Whether it's "Destination Disease," "Someone Sickness," or a bad case of "The Backward Blues," many people are waiting for something, some change, some do-over, or some person, before they believe they can be happy. But the truth is there's something that can bring you more joy right now than getting something you don't have. That something is being grateful for what you do have.

Dale Carnegie was once interviewed by television producer and anthologist Leonard Safir. Safir asked Carnegie: What's the secret to being happy? In the course of the conversation, money came up. How much money did it take to be happy?

Carnegie asked Safir if he thought a million dollars would him happy. "Sure, of course," the reporter responded. Carnegie continued, "Would you sell both your eyes for a million dollars…or your two legs…or your hands…or your hearing? Add up what you do have, and you'll find that you won't sell them for all the gold in the world. The best things in life are yours."[4]

Why do we believe something we don't have will make us happy when we already possess more valuable blessings yet struggle to be content? The best things in life are yours already.

What would you take in exchange for your health? What's more important to you than your children and other loved ones? How valuable is it to you to live in a country where you're free to speak your mind and do what you desire? What price would you put on your salvation? The best things in life are yours already. Right now you have more than enough to be grateful and full of joy.

Here's a promise I can make to you: Become fixated on what you don't have and unhappiness will flood your life. But develop the "attitude of gratitude" and you will begin to experience real joy. When you wake up in the morning, think of five blessing that are yours and thank God for them. As you go to sleep, review your day and identify at least one gift that God brought into your life and express your gratitude to God.

You will discover that the best things in life are yours, and you will find that you have more than enough to be filled with joy.

4. We must get our faith right.

Paul believed that God knew him and loved him. Paul believed that God was committed to him and that God was at work in his life. He encouraged the Philippians to believe the same things. "Work hard to show the results of your salvation, obeying God with deep reverence and fear. For God is working in you, giving you the desire and the power to do what pleases him" (Philippians 2:12-13 NLT).

When life becomes difficult, Paul tells the Philippians not to give up, give in, or get down. Why? Because "God is working in you."

Look at the lives of history's great men and women and you will find that almost all of them had times when they were tempted to give up their dreams, throw in the towel, and live small lives. That's true in the secular world, and it's true of men and women who accomplished great things in the Bible.

Here's another common denominator. Most of those men and women would tell you that it was during those difficult times that they learned the lessons that prepared them for their later success. It was in the furnace of their trials that their faith was forged. It was in the midst of their struggles that their character was strengthened. It was in the times when they wondered where

God was that later they looked back on as the moment when God was doing his greatest work in their lives.

Malcolm Muggeridge lived one of the most interesting lives of the twentieth century. During World War II, he was a British soldier and spy. Later he was a journalist and author. At one time a left-wing sympathizer, he became a staunch anti-communist. And late in life, after covering the work of Mother Teresa, the formerly agnostic Muggeridge committed his life to Christ.

Toward the end of his life, Muggeridge was interviewed by William Buckley, who brought up the topic of suffering. Muggeridge responded by saying that when we look back on life, we realize the only thing that has taught us anything is suffering. What teaches us what life is really about, he said, is affliction.[5]

Hard times can make us stronger. Suffering can make us wise. Going without can make us appreciate all we have. Trials can make us more like Christ. I want to invite you to believe what Paul believed about God. You are not in this world alone. There is a divine power and a divine Person who is committed to you. He is working to make you wise, giving you strength, and creating in you the character needed to succeed at what matters most in life.

Let life do its worst. Let it take your job, your health, your dreams, even your loved ones. But don't ever let it take away from you the certainty that God is at work in your life. Believe as Paul did that even if you are imprisoned and in pain, you are not alone. God is with you. He will have the last word over your life and that word will be good.

5. We must get our purpose right.

One reason many people are unhappy and unfulfilled is because the purpose they're living for is too small. They've sold themselves short. There's something in them that yearns for more.

In the Book of Ecclesiastes we are told that God "has also set eternity in the human heart" (3:11). There is something within us that wants to live for a purpose that matters—a purpose that will make a difference in this world and in the world to come. No matter how much of this world's pleasures and prizes we may acquire, it will never be enough to bring the joy Jesus prayed we would know. True, lasting joy comes only when the One who is eternal lives within us and we are living for a purpose that will matter forever. Until we do, we will always find ourselves longing for something more, wondering why we can have everything this world offers and still find ourselves empty inside.

Fail to live for a great purpose, and you may find yourself able to identify with what Ed Sissman wrote in a poem about men over the age of forty who wake up at night and find themselves looking out at the city lights, wondering where they went wrong and "why life is so long."[6]

There are many ways to describe what our purpose is. Here in Philippians, Paul says to "become blameless and pure, 'children of God without fault in a warped and crooked generation.' Then you will shine among them like stars in the sky as you hold firmly to the word of life" (Philippians 2:15b-16a).

What's our purpose? It's to bring light to people who are in darkness. It's to bring light to those who are lost and lonely, who are hurting and desperate, who are struggling and longing for hope. It's to bring light to people who are confused because the world has lied to them about who they are, what God is like, what's true, and what's right. We are here to care enough about those people that we enter their world and with our words and our deeds bring light into their lives.

Robert Fulghum was a best-selling author in the 1980s and '90s. In *It Was on Fire When I Lay Down on It*, he writes that at the end of every lecture he attends, if he is given the opportunity, he asks a question. It's always the same question. Regardless of the topic that has been discussed, he asks the presenter, "What's the meaning of life?" His question is almost always met with laughter by the others in the audience, and the speaker usually takes that as a cue to dismiss the crowd.

One time was different. Dr. Fulghum was attending a conference on the island of Crete hosted by an institute dedicated to fostering understanding and reconciliation among people of different cultures. The institute's founder, Dr. Alexander Papaderos, stood in the sunlight of an open window and asked for questions. Fulghum raised his hand and asked his question, "What is the meaning of life?" People began to laugh and some got up to leave, but Papaderos motioned for people to be seated as he looked closely at the questioner.

Believing he discerned a sincere heart, Papaderos reached into a pocket, took out his wallet, and then removed from it a small, round mirror about the size of a quarter. He told the audience that he had grown up poor in a remote village. As a boy during World War II, he had come upon a place where a German motorcycle had wrecked. Its mirror was shattered. The largest piece, "this one," Papaderos said, he picked up, then he smoothed the rough edges and rounded it off into a circle.

He became fascinated by the way he was able to reflect light into the darkest of places—deep holes, the corners of closets, places that before had never seen the light of the sun. The more inaccessible the place, the more joy he received by bringing the light there.

Papaderos kept the mirror with him as he grew older, continuing his little game, until he realized that it was in fact a metaphor of what he was to do with his life. He told Fulghum and the others who listened to him, "I came to understand that I am not the light. . . . But light—truth, understanding, knowledge—is there, and it will only shine in many dark places if I reflect it. . . . I can reflect light into the dark places of this world . . . and change some things in some people. . . . This is the meaning of my life."

Then Dr. Papaderos held up his mirror and moved it slightly so that the sunlight from the window fell upon Robert Fulghum's face.[7]

The world that God loves is lost, broken, and hurting. His great purpose in Jesus Christ was to bring grace and truth into the world so that all might be forgiven, healed, and restored into a right relationship with him. In some way, we must become a part of what God is doing in the world. His purpose, his good purpose for the world he loves, must become our purpose. In some way, we must shine into the darkness of this world so that those who are lost can find their way to God.

Living for an eternal purpose will not make your life easy. It will make you care about people who are hurting when others are able to see the same needs you see and walk away without a second thought. It will make you lay down your life and sacrifice what others hold dear. It will force you to keep going when you are tired and to keep giving when you feel you have come to the end of yourself.

Loving the world God loves and being a light in the darkness will not make your life easy. But it will make your life good. And when you love in this way, you will no longer have to run off looking for joy, because joy will have found you.

NOTES

Chapter 1

1. "Tom Hanks Movie Career Salaries," Statistic Brain, http://www
   .statisticbrain.com/tom-hanks-career-earnings/, accessed November
   20, 2017.
2. "Tom Hanks Says Self-Doubt Is 'A High-Wire Act That We
   All Walk,'" *NPR: Fresh Air*, April 26, 2016, https://www.npr
   .org/2016/04/26/475573489/tom-hanks-says-self-doubt-is-a-high
   -wire-act-that-we-all-walk, accessed November 20, 2017.
3. "Origin of Anxious," from *Webster's New World College Dictionary*,
   Fifth Edition; Copyright 2014 by Houghton Mifflin Harcourt
   Publishing Company, http://www.yourdictionary.com/anxious,
   accessed November 20, 2017.
4. "Worry," Online Etymology Dicitonary, http://www.etymonline.com
   /index.php?term=worry, accessed November 20, 2017.
5. Ralph W. Sockman, *The Higher Happiness* (Nashville: Abingdon,
   1950), 15.
6. Emily Maust Wood, "20 Powerful Quotes from Charles Spurgeon,"
   Crosswalk.com, http://www.crosswalk.com/faith/spiritual-life
   /inspiring-quotes/20-powerful-quotes-from-charles-spurgeon.html,
   accessed November 20, 2017.
7. Julia Cameron, *Finding Water: The Art of Perseverance* (New York:
   TarcherPerigee, 2009), 128.
8. Robert Hastings, *The Station: A Reminder to Cherish the Journey*
   (Golden Valley, MN: Tristan Publishing, 2003).
9. Sir William Osler, *Osler's "A Way of Life" and Other Addresses, with
   Commentary and Annotations*, ed. Shigeaki Hinohara and Hisae Niki
   (Durham & London: Duke University Press, 2001), 6.
10. Ibid.

11. Sidney Lanier, "The Marshes of Glynn," Poets.org, https://www.poets
.org/poetsorg/poem/marshes-glynn, accessed November 20, 2017.
12. Ibid.
13. Julia Cameron, *Finding Water*, 128.

Chapter 2

1. Frederick Buechner, *Wishful Thinking: A Seeker's ABC* (New York:
HarperCollins, 1993), 2.
2. Rudolf Bultmann, "*Aphiēmi*," in *Theological Dictionary of the New
Testament*, vol. 1, ed. Gerhard Kittel and Geoffrey W. Bromiley, trans.
Geoffrey W. Bromiley (Grand Rapids: Eerdmans, 1964), 509–512.
3. Antwone Q. Fisher, *Who Will Cry for the Little Boy? Poems* (New
York: HarperCollins, 2003), 1.
4. Aristotle, *The Nicomachean Ethics*, trans. J. A. K. Thomson and Hugh
Tredennick (New York: Penguin Classics, 2004), Book II, 49.
5. Lewis B. Smedes, *Shame and Grace: Healing the Shame We Don't
Deserve* (San Francisco: HarperSanFrancisco/Zondervan, 1993), 141.
6. "Woman survives being sexually assaulted, strangled and doused in
bleach as she escapes killer who put teen's body in freezer," *Daily
Mail*, November 11, 2011, http://www.dailymail.co.uk/news
/article-2059949/Lydia-Tillman-escapes-killer-Travis-Forbes-Kenia
-Monges-body-freezer.html, accessed November 20, 2017.
7. *Carter v. Rafferty*, U.S. District Court D. New Jersey, November 7,
1985, http://www.leagle.com/decision/19851154621FSupp533_11085
.xml/CARTER%20v.%20RAFFERTY, accessed November 20, 2017.
8. Rubin Carter, quoted in James S. Hirsch, *Hurricane: The Miraculous
Journey of Rubin Carter* (Boston: Houghton Mifflin, 2000), 310.

Chapter 3

1. Frank Minirth and Paul Meier, *Happiness is a Choice: The Symptoms,
Causes, and Cures of Depression*, Updated Edition (Grand Rapids:
Baker, 2007), 107.
2. Mark Twain, *Following the Equator: A Journey Around the World*,
vol. 1 (New York: Harper and Brothers, 1897), 125.
3. Minda Zetlin, "Listening to Complainers Is Bad for Your Brain," *Inc.
Magazine*, August 20, 2012, https://www.inc.com/minda-zetlin
/listening-to-complainers-is-bad-for-your-brain.html, accessed
November 20, 2017.

4. University of Warwick Press Release, "Study suggests you can 'pick up' a good or bad mood from your friends," September 20, 2017, https://www2.warwick.ac.uk/newsandevents/pressreleases/study _suggests_you/, accessed November 20, 2017.

Chapter 4

1. James Allen, *As We Think, So We Are: James Allen's Guide to Transforming Our Lives*, ed. Ruth L. Miller (New York: Atria/Beyond Words, 2012), 221.
2. "Everyone who has ever taken a shower has had a good idea. The thing that matters is what you do with that idea once you get out of the shower." Nolan Bushnell with Gene Stone, *Finding the Next Steve Jobs: How to Find, Keep, and Nurture Creative Talent* (New York: Simon and Schuster, 2013), 224.
3. Jules Renard, *The Journal of Jules Renard* (New York: Tin House Books, 2008), 85.
4. Darrin McMahon, quoted in Carolyn Gregoire, "How Happiness Became a Cultural Obsession," *The Huffington Post*, March 20, 2014, http://www.huffingtonpost.com/2014/03/20/happiness-self -help_n_4979780.html, accessed November 20, 2017.
5. Ruth Whippman, *America the Anxious: How Our Pursuit of Happiness Is Creating a Nation of Nervous Wrecks* (New York: St. Martin's Press, 2016), 9.
6. Ibid., 36.
7. Ibid., 10.
8. Adrian Furnham, "The Dark Side of Happiness," *Psychology Today*, February 19, 2014, https://www.psychologytoday.com/blog/sideways -view/201402/the-dark-side-happiness, accessed November 20, 2017.
9. Iris B. Mauss, Maya Tamir, Craig L. Anderson, and Nicole S. Savino, "Can Seeking Happiness Make People Happy? Paradoxical Effects of Valuing Happiness," *Emotion* 11(4) (2011), 807–815. https://www .ncbi.nlm.nih.gov/pmc/articles/PMC3160511/, accessed December 5, 2017.
10. George Bernard Shaw, *Man and Superman: A Comedy and a Philosophy*, Epistle Dedicatory (New York: Brentano's, 1922), xxxi-xxxii.

11. George Bernard Shaw, "Art and Public Money," published in the *Sussex Daily News* (7 March 1907), http://shawquotations .blogspot.com/2014/08/life-is-no-brief-candle-to-me.html, accessed December 5, 2017.

Chapter 5

1. C. S. Lewis, *Mere Christianity* (New York: HarperOne, 2001), 16.
2. *Augustine of Hippo, Selected Writings*, trans. Mary T. Clark (Mahwah, NJ: Paulist Press, 1984), 291.

Chapter 6

1. John Milton, *Paradise Lost*, bk. 1, lines 254–255. https://www .dartmouth.edu/~milton/reading_room/pl/book_1/text.shtml, accessed December 6, 2017.
2. Lewis Thomas, *The Medusa and the Snail: More Notes of a Biology Watcher* (New York: Penguin Books, 1995), 4–5.
3. John Maxwell writes about Destination Disease in "What I Believe about Success," March 5, 2014, http://www.johnmaxwell.com/blog /what-i-believe-about-success, accessed November 20, 2017. He writes about Someone Sickness in *Developing the Leader Within You* (Nashville: Thomas Nelson, 1993), 105.
4. William Safire and Leonard Safir, eds., *Words of Wisdom: More Good Advice* (New York: Simon and Schuster, 1989), 399.
5. "Firing Line with William F. Buckley Jr.: How Does One Find Faith?," September 6, 1980, Firing Line broadcast records, 59:20, Hoover Institution Archives, https://digitalcollections.hoover.org /objects/6608, accessed December 18, 2017.
6. L. E. Sissman, *Night Music: Poems* (New York: Houghton Mifflin, 1999), 58.
7. Robert Fulghum, *It Was on Fire When I Lay Down on It* (New York: Ivy Books, 1988), 173–175.